INTERWEAVE.
interweavebooks.com

Knitting Socks *with* Handpainted Yarn

Carol Sulcoski

Editor, Anne Merrow
Technical editor, Kristen TenDyke
Photography, Joe Coca
Photo stylist, Ann Swanson
Cover design, Connie Poole
Layout design, Bonnie Brooks

Interweave Press LLC
201 East Fourth Street
Loveland, CO 80537-5655 USA
interweavebooks.com

Printed in China through Asia Pacific Offset.

Library of Congress Cataloging-in-Publication Data

Sulcoski, Carol, 1965-
  Knitting socks with handpainted yarn / Carol Sulcoski, author.
     p. cm.
  Includes index.
  ISBN 978-1-59668-098-2 (pbk.)
  1. Knitting--Patterns. 2. Socks. I. Title.
  TT820.S935 2009
  746.43'2--dc22

                              2008020565

10 9 8 7 6 5 4 3 2 1

To my husband, Tom, who only rarely complains that I never knit him socks yet who certainly deserves an entire wardrobe of them.

Acknowledgments

My deepest appreciation to the wonderful designers who submitted such creative and beautiful patterns (and who worked within a tight deadline); to super test knitters Mindy Soucek and Kristi Geraci; to my editor Anne Merrow, who is a true pleasure to work with and improved this book immeasurably; to technical editor Kristen TenDyke, for her attention to detail; to Rebecca Campbell and her beautiful feet; to Joe Coca, for his lovely photographs; to my knitting and non-knitting friends for their support and encouragement; and to my children, James, Nick, and Grace, for being so darn cute and fun.

Thanks to Rosie's Yarn Cellar for supplying yarn and to Sheri of The Loopy Ewe for overnighting an emergency skein without question.

But my greatest debt is owed to all of the clever knitters throughout the ages who figured out how to create and improve the marvel of engineering that is the handknit sock.

contents

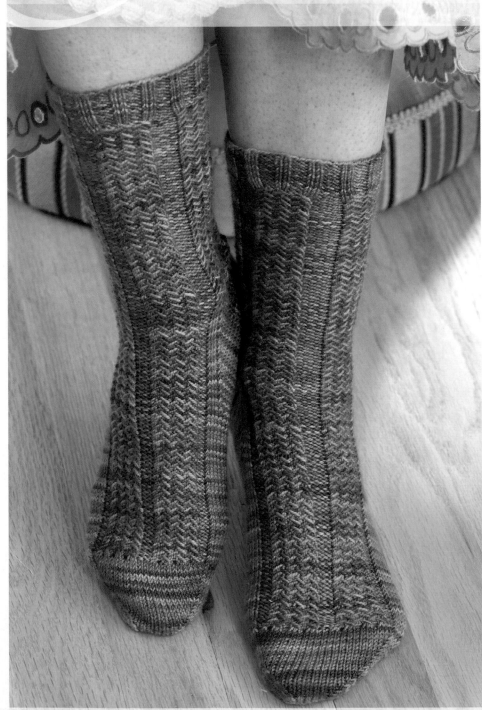

The Road to Handpainted Happiness

Handpainted sock yarns...

They hypnotize us with spectacular hues, beguile us with unusual color combinations, and tempt us with their luscious fibers. We wait in line for them at fiber shows, we subscribe to Internet waiting lists for them, we join sock clubs to be sure that we won't miss out on our favorites. You may have a sizeable stash of them tucked away in a bin (or several bins) in a closet. It's no wonder that handpainted sock yarn has been described as "crack for knitters."

Yet as much as we love handpainted yarns, they may frustrate us, too. How many times have you started knitting a sock with a skein of handpainted yarn that you love, only to rip it out in disappointment because it just doesn't look the way you hoped it would? Maybe the colors looked great in the hank but not so good knitted up. Maybe the colors formed displeasing patterns, zigzagging or swirling or making irregular blotches. Maybe the stitch pattern you were working so hard to perfect was drowned out by multiple colors fighting for attention.

This book is for every knitter who has eagerly started a pair of socks in handpainted yarn, then wanted to rip them out in dissatisfaction. Start by learning more about handpainted yarns, including how to predict their behavior and how to avoid undesirable color effects like pooling. Once you thoroughly understand the way handpainted yarns work, dive in and knit one of the twenty-one sock patterns with a surer sense of how to select the right pattern for the specific yarn you're using. Before you know it, you'll have a wardrobe of beautiful, unique socks that are as fun and satisfying to knit as they are to wear.

Before You Start

This book assumes that you already know how to knit a basic sock. Although the vast majority of the patterns are written for double-pointed needles, you can, of course, use other techniques (like two circular needles or one long circular needle) if you wish. If you haven't yet knitted a sock, take a class at your local yarn shop, get a knitting friend to teach you how, or consult a reference like *Getting Started Knitting Socks* by Ann Budd to learn the basics. These resources can also help you adapt patterns written for double-pointed needles for use with other types of needles. The focus here is on the yarn: understanding handpaints and why they behave the way they do when knit into socks.

Most sock yarns are fingering weight, knitting at around 7 to 8 stitches per inch (Super Fine #1, in the Craft Yarn Council's Standard Weight System; see below), so most of the patterns in this book are written for yarn at this gauge.

Finally, it bears repeating that hand-dyed yarns are by their very nature unique. Different dyelots of the same colorway can look remarkably different; even different skeins within the same dyelot can look more like fraternal than identical twins. Even if you purchase one of the yarns used for the samples in this book in the same colorway shown, realize that your skein may not look exactly the same as the photograph. Embrace the individuality of the yarn, rather than worrying too much about having it "match."

About Multicolored Yarns

Space-dyed, hand-dyed, handpainted, nearly solid—you've probably heard all these terms and more when browsing for yarn. What do these terms mean? And do any of those distinctions matter when all you want to do is knit a good-looking pair of socks?

You bet. Learning a bit of background about multicolored sock yarns can pay big dividends when it comes time to select them for your sock projects. So let's start with some basics.

Hand-Dyed vs Machine-Dyed Yarns

It's a completely obvious point, but one worth making: some yarns are dyed by hand, while others are dyed by machine. Hey, you're saying, this is a book about hand-dyed yarns, right? So why are we even talking about machine-dyed yarns?

Well, it sometimes isn't easy to tell the difference between yarns that are hand-dyed and yarns dyed by machine. Yarn companies can produce machine-dyed yarns that closely resemble handpaints. Using a mechanized

Yarn Size	Needle Size	Gauge (stitches/4" [10 cm])
#0 Lace (thread)	U.S. 000–1 1.5–2.25 mm	33–40
#1 Super Fine (fingering)	U.S. 1–3 2.25–3.25 mm	27–32
#2 Fine (sport)	U.S. 3–5 3.25–3.75 mm	23–26
#3 Light (DK)	U.S. 5–7 3.75–4.5 mm	21–24
#4 Medium (worsted)	U.S. 7–9 3.75–5.5 mm	16–20
#5 Bulky (chunky)	U.S. 9–11 5.5–8 mm	12–15

The different effects in these handpainted skeins are made with a variety of dyeing techniques.

process called space-dyeing, different colors of dye are applied along the strands of yarn at regular or semi-regular intervals. The space-dyeing process produces a multicolored yarn that can resemble the variegated hues of your favorite handpaints. Why choose space-dyed, as opposed to hand-dyed, yarns? Cost is one reason: because the dye is applied by machines rather than artisans, space-dyed yarns are often (though not always) cheaper than hand-dyed yarns. If you're on a budget, you may be able to achieve a similar look to handpainted yarn at a lower price by opting for a space-dyed yarn.

Another reason is consistency. Because space-dyed yarns are produced by a machine rather than a human, they may tend to be more consistent or uniform in their colors and color patterns. (This isn't always true; as many knitters can tell you to their sorrow, even solid-colored yarns can vary a great deal between dyelots, and multicolored yarns, which use more colors, present greater opportunity for color variation.) As a general rule, hand-dyed yarns tend to show much greater variation in the colors they use and in the way dye is applied to the yarn, creating greater differences among colorways and dyelots. If that kind of unpredictability stresses you out rather than exhilarates you, you may enjoy working with space-dyed yarns that aren't quite so idiosyncratic.

Of course, the same thing that makes handpaints so unpredictable is, for many people, the thrill of working with them: no two skeins are exactly alike, and even two socks knit in the same pattern from the same dyelot of the same yarn may turn out looking dramatically different.

Luckily, it doesn't have to be one or the other: you can fall in love with space-dyed and hand-dyed yarns, and the patterns and techniques in this book will help you have fun with both.

Because hand-dyed yarns have greater—often substantial—variations between skeins and dyelots, it's especially important to purchase sufficient yarn to complete your project, as it may be impossible to find a close match to your dyelot should you run out later.

 FIBERS

The most common fiber used for hand-dyed sock yarn is wool. Wool has many advantages for the hand-dyer and the sock knitter: it dyes easily and well, and the dyer has more choices for suitable dyes than fibers derived from plants; it's from a renewable resource; it's elastic, it's warm and durable; it often comes in superwash versions. Merino yarn is a favorite of hand-dyers because it's soft enough for next-to-the skin wear and it takes dye well, but other types of wool such as Blue-faced Leicester are becoming more readily available. Wool socks aren't necessarily too hot to wear year-round; I find that my wool socks are comfortable a good nine months or more in my mid-Atlantic climate, and they are always a good choice for wearing under hiking boots.

Because of the heavy wear that socks get, many commercially dyed yarns are made with a component of nylon or polyamide, man-made fibers that give extra durability and strength to the yarn. If you're prone to wear holes in your heels or toes, wool/nylon blends are a good choice for sturdy socks.

The influx of new fiber blends in handpainted yarns is especially exciting. As fibers like bamboo and Tencel (lyocell) have become more widely available, dyers have begun to source undyed hanks of these blends and produce gorgeous hand-dyed skeins. Hand-dyed sock yarns containing lyocell (a fiber derived from wood pulp), bamboo, silk, cotton, and SeaCell (a fiber derived in part from seaweed) are now readily available at fiber festivals, in some yarn shops, and via the Internet.

*Self-striping
hand-dyed yarns*

Different Kinds of Hand-Dyed Yarns

Leaving aside space-dyed yarns for now, let's consider the hand-dyed ones. The most common description you're likely to hear when looking at hand-dyed yarns is that a particular yarn was "handpainted." The term "hand-painted" refers to a specific method of applying dye to a yarn. Traditionally, hand-dyed yarns are made when the dyer uses a brush (a bristled brush or a foam one), sponge, or some other implement to "paint" the dye onto the individual strands of yarn. Using a brush gives the dyer more control over the dye, including the ability to create short segments of color that morph into one another.

Not all hand-dyed yarns are made by the process of painting, however. Dyers have shown remarkable ingenuity in inventing their own methods of applying dye to yarn by hand, including:

- Squirting or pouring dye directly onto the fiber. Some dyers apply dye very carefully and in a controlled way using plastic bottles with nozzles or syringes; others pour or even slosh it on, overlapping colors and creating blended effects; some dyers fling droplets of dye to get splotches or dots of color.

- Immersion (or kettle) dyeing, in which a receptacle (a bowl, a large pot, or a vat) is filled with a dye solution, and the skeins of yarn are dunked in the dye. The skein can be immersed entirely or only partway. Immersion dyeing produces yarns that are nearly solid, perhaps with variations in the lightness or darkness of the shade.

- Dip-dyeing, in which sections of yarn are dipped into containers of dye but the entire skein is not submersed in any one color of dye.

- Combining one or more of the above methods with overdyeing, e.g., applying a first round of color using one of the above techniques, then immersing the entire skein into a dyebath, altering the colors that were originally applied and coloring any remaining white sections.

There isn't any one technique that is "better" than the others; each can create beautiful and unique skeins of yarn for knitters to enjoy. For purposes of this book, however, we're going to use the term "handpaint" loosely, to include any of the techniques for applying multiple colors by hand to a skein of yarn.

Self-Patterning and Self-Striping Yarns

Before we dive headlong into the world of handpainted multis, it's worth talking about a special kind of hand-painted yarn. Clever dyers have figured out ways to create yarns that make specific, intentional patterns, rather than random changes of color. The most common kind of self-patterning hand-dyed yarn is yarn that automatically stripes. The striping may be abrupt, with the beginning and end of each color very distinct; or the colors may flow into each other, with gradations in color changing slowly as one shade morphs into another. The stripes may be thick bands of color, with each stripe lasting for several rounds of your sock, or they may be thinner bands that last the length of only one or two rounds. Occasionally you'll even find a hand-dyer who plays around with more complicated patterns, like the jacquard or checkerboard styles that you often see in commercially dyed yarn; however, this is such an exacting and labor-intensive process, only the most intrepid hand-dyers go there.

How can you tell the difference between a yarn that will stripe and a yarn that will not? I'll talk a bit more about this in the section on repeats (see page 17), but for now, take comfort in the fact that most hand-dyers who delib-erately create self-striping yarn will tell you up front—and they'll likely charge you a bit more per skein for it, since the process involves extra yarn handling.

What do you do if you find a ball of self-striping yarn in your stash? Well, self-striping yarns tend to be pretty easy to handle. The stripes make a regular pattern, instead of the random splotches of color that non-striping hand-dyes make. You may decide that knitting the sock in a simple stockinette or rib stitch is just fine, letting the yarn do its magic and stripe as it will. You may decide a pattern with some sort of horizontal patterning show-cases the horizontal changes of color, or you may opt for a chevron stitch, which can create zigs and zags of color as the stripes develop. Self-striping yarns tend to be less bewildering to the knitter, though, because the colors and stripes play out over several rows in simple and predictable blocks or lines of color.

Since the majority of hand-dyed sock yarns you'll encounter do not have any deliberately created patterning or stripes, we've chosen to focus on non-patterned yarns in this book. They may be called "multicolors," or "varie-gated," or simply "handpaints." Let's take a closer look at how they operate.

Handpainted skeins
from wild to mild to
somewhere in between

Class by Color

One of the things we most love about hand-dyes are their colors: unique shades or creative combinations of shades. But sometimes all that color can seem overwhelming. How do you know how to match a colorway to a sock pattern? When are all those colors just too much? When is it worth laboring over a stitch pattern and when is it better to do something plain?

You don't have to have an art degree or a background in color theory to figure out how to use handpainted yarns. You just need a good framework for analyzing your yarns and a little practice in applying it. Let's start by looking at some examples of handpainted sock yarns.

The three skeins of sock yarn above are all hand-dyed. They vary a great deal in their appearance, however, ranging from the subtle to the dramatic. Begin by taking a close look at each skein and count the number of distinct colors you see in each one. Don't drive yourself too crazy; this exercise isn't meant to challenge you to name each color in the crayon box, drawing painterly distinctions between red-orange and orange-red, or burnt umber vs raw umber. But when you look at each skein, do you see a skein that is mostly one color, but with many shades of that color? Do you see a skein that has two or three different colors, but no more than that? Or do you see a skein that has more than three distinct colors in it, a veritable spectrum of shades?

Consider the middle skein: it's dyed entirely in shades of periwinkle blue. Some areas are lighter and some are darker, but all are a variation of the same shade of light purplish-blue. Compare the periwinkle skein to the skein at the bottom of the photo; the lower skein was dyed in a riot of bright colors, including red, yellow, orange, and green. And the skein at the top? There is a main color, blue—several shades of it—along with two other colors, pink and purple. It's definitely got more than one color, unlike the periwinkle blue skein, but it doesn't have nearly as many hues as the bottom skein.

Each of these skeins of sock yarn uses color differently, and the distinct ways that each uses color hints at how best to knit it up. So when you first contemplate knitting a pair of socks from a skein of handpainted yarn, take a few minutes (maybe while you're winding it into a ball?) to study the colors. See if you can categorize the skein as we did above as a Nearly Solid; a Wild Multi; or a Muted Multi.

Nearly Solids

Wild Multis

Nearly Solids

This category consists of skeins that are entirely one color. They may contain lighter or darker shades of that color, or shades that are very close but just a hair different from that color.

Not all handpainted yarn companies make Nearly Solids; some brands that do are Koigu, Dream in Color, Lorna's Laces Shepherd Sock, Araucania Ranco Semi-Solids, Shibui Knits, Blue Moon Fiber Arts, and Nature's Palette. Usually if a brand comes in both solids and multis, the solids will be clearly labeled as "solids," "semi-solids," or "nearly solids" as opposed to "multis."

Because they feature substantially less variation in color (indeed, some are very solid), the knitter has a great deal of flexibility when knitting with them. Most patterns will show up well, particularly in lighter colorways, and the relative uniformity of color won't distract the eye from your stitchwork. Generally speaking, this is where you're best advised to do fancier stitches—cables, textured patterns, lace.

Wild Multis

If the Nearly Solids are at the subtle end of the continuum, Wild Multis fall squarely at the other. Wild Multis are just what they sound like: yarns that contain multiple colors, unusual shades, creative combinations, or vivid or deep colors. Wild Multis aren't everyone's cup of tea: some people find the disjointed nature of the colors jarring, and I've even heard them described disparagingly as "clown barf." But if you love color, Wild Multis are a jolt of visual adrenaline. As I do more and more dyeing, I appreciate Wild Multis more and more. I enjoy seeing fresh combinations of shades, and I find that knitting or putting on wildly colored socks is a pick-me-up on cold, dark winter days.

You'll find Wild Multis in many popular hand-dyed yarn lines, particularly the ones by indie dyers; some specific examples shown above are (clockwise from lower left) Lorna's Laces, Koigu, Schaefer, Blue Moon Fiber Arts, and No No Kitty Yarns. Wild Multis are the most challenging to work with, and it's here that knitters seem to experience the most frustration. Colors that look pleasing in the hank can look quite different when knit up, and effects like pooling and splotching can dominate the finished socks in a way the knitter didn't intend. The general rule is that the

Muted Multis

brighter the colors and the more colors used, the more the yarn will fight with your stitches. Using simpler patterns with these ensures that stitch patterns or designs don't get drowned out by the quickly changing colors. Fear not; later in this book, you'll find several patterns specifically designed to work well with even the toughest Wild Multis.

Muted Multis

Muted Multis fall in the middle of the hand-dyed yarn spectrum. These skeins contain two or three different colors but create an overall effect that is fairly restrained.

You may find a skein that is mainly one shade, with short bursts of contrasting colors spaced fairly far apart. Or a skein may contain only two colors, like the blue and white skein on the right. There are variations in those colors—redder pinks and more lilac pinks, plums and violets and indigos—but overall, the effect isn't garish or overwhelming because all the individual shades are closely related. You may even find a skein that has more than two colors, like the light shades in the skein second from the right, but the colors are closely related in hue or shade.

The thing to remember about Muted Multis is that the colors mesh together well. There aren't too many colors, the colors that are there don't clash, and no single color dominates your eye or drowns out the others. They are the workhorses of the handpainted yarn world. Muted Multi colorways shown here (from left to right) are from Black

Bunny Fibers, three skeins of Koigu, and Shibui Sock.

When it comes to knitting with Muted Multis, there are a lot of choices (though not as many as with Nearly Solids). You'll want to stay away from the most complicated patterns; extremely intricate lace or cables, for example, may get lost or minimized by the differences in color or hue. But you can play around with interesting patterns and textures. Many of the patterns in this book were designed to work well with Muted Multis, using eyelets, lace, ribbing, cables, and other techniques to shuffle the colors around while allowing you to have fun with some stitchwork.

Two More Color Tips

If you take nothing else away from this discussion but how to divide your handpaints into Nearly Solids, Muted Multis, and Wild Multis, and select sock patterns accordingly, you'll have much more success—and fun!—with your handpainted socks. But understanding color is more complicated than that, and if you want to be the master of your handpaints, there are two more facets of color theory that you should have a nodding acquaintance with before you pick up those knitting needles. (If you find yourself intrigued by color theory, an excellent reference applying color theory to fiber arts is *ColorWorks: The Crafter's Guide to Color* by Deb Menz.)

Converting a color photograph to black and white shows the value.

Value: The Black-and-White TV

Value can be a tough concept to get your mind around. The most common way to explain value is that it measures how light or dark a color is, when compared to a scale of gray tones. What finally hammered home the concept of value to me, though, was to think of a black-and-white television. When you watch a show on a black-and-white television, you don't see different hues: there's no brown or yellow or blue, only shades of gray. But there is much diversity in those shades of gray; they range from very light to very dark, with every permutation in between. These varying shades of gray are comparable to a color's value.

How can something so hard to describe be so important? Well, even though value isn't something you might immediately think about, it's something that your eyes immediately notice. In fact, from farther away, your eyes will notice differences in value more than they will notice differences in hue. Suppose you have a skein of sock yarn that consists of beige, dark brown, and several shades of taupe and sage. When you look at this yarn, your eyes will tend to focus on the contrast between the beige areas (the lightest color, the one that would look like palest gray on the black-and-white set) and the dark brown areas (the darkest color, the one that would look like charcoal or almost black on the black-and-white television). The middle tones, the taupes and sages, will take a backseat to the sharp contrast between the lightest color and the darkest.

If you have trouble parsing out which colors have a light value and which have a dark value, take advantage of modern technology. Take a digital photo of the yarn—and ideally a swatch of the yarn knitted up—and display it on your computer monitor. Then use a photo viewing program or your monitor's settings to turn off the color, creating the same kind of black-and-white image as the old black-and-white television sets. You should be able to see the varying shades of gray. Are they all on the light side? All on the dark side? Or all in the middle ranges? Are there lots of variations in light, medium, and dark?

What does this mean when it comes to knitting with handpaints? The most important principle to remember is that the more variations in value, and the greater the variations within a single skein, the simpler your stitch pattern should be. With subtler variations in value, you'll have more flexibility in getting fancy with texture and patterning.

Saturation: How Bright Is My Handpaint

The last concept to think about when analyzing your handpainted yarn is saturation. Saturation can be described as how intense a color is, how bright or dull it is, or how strong it is. A color like traffic-cone orange is saturated and intense; it's a color that calls out to you (or in some cases, screams at you). A color like petal pink is not very saturated; it whispers.

I bet you can see where this is going: the more intense or saturated a color is, the more it's going to dominate the skein of yarn (or the finished pair of socks). Even a little bit of a very intense color will draw the eye and may drown out other, less saturated (quieter) shades. It's sometimes said that intense colors make each other look even more intense: juxtaposing lime green and hot fuchsia pink and turquoise will make each of those colors seem brighter and more vivid. Putting lime green next to low-intensity colors like taupe or gray will make the low-intensity colors seem duller.

Very saturated colors can be like the one singer with the really strong voice in a choir: even though every member of the choir is singing the same song, your ear can't escape that one soprano with the exceptionally strong voice that soars above the rest. If your skein has lots of saturated colors, they will tend to dominate the knitting, overwhelming other, less-saturated colors and drowning out intricate patterns. Even small shots of saturated color can jump out at you, drawing your eye away from the rest of the yarn's hues.

Color Me Confident

Thoroughly bewildered by now? Don't be. Here's a checklist that you can use to analyze all the handpainted yarns in your stash. The answers will direct you to the kinds of patterns you should use. (See page 25 for symbol key.)

1. IS THE SKEIN A NEARLY SOLID, A MUTED MULTI, OR A WILD MULTI? If the answer is "Nearly Solid," go find a fun stitch pattern and have at it. Patterns marked with the "Nearly Solid" symbol are great for nearly solid yarns. If you've got a multi, continue below.

2. IF THE SKEIN IS A MULTI, DOES THE SKEIN HAVE LOTS OF VARIATIONS IN COLOR, VALUE, OR INTENSITY? If the answer is no, then take a middle ground: some stitch patterning or texture will work, but don't go overboard. The patterns in this book marked with the "Muted Multi" symbol will give you some good choices if you feel unsure where to begin. If the answer to any of these is yes, then tread softly. Use a simple stitch pattern, or try some of the patterns marked with the "Wild Multi" symbol. (See symbols on page 25.)

Repeats—or Why You Get Pooling, Splotching, and Other Weird Patterns

Wait just a minute! I know you're eager to dive into applying all your newfound color theory, but there's one more thing you've got to know. In fact, it's so important that you really shouldn't cast on until you understand it! It's the idea of repeats, and it's your key to understanding—and avoiding—striping, pooling, and other effects commonly seen with handpainted yarns.

Knitting-related message boards are full of distraught posts that sound something like this:

Help! I'm knitting my first sock in a handpainted yarn. I'm partway down the leg and I hate it! The colors are making this weird pattern, kind of splotchy (or zigzag, or stripy). Is there anything I can do to change this? The yarn wasn't cheap and I loved it in the skein, but I hate how this sock looks!

Knitters use a lot of different terms to describe this syndrome: pooling, splotching, stacking, and striping are a few. Basically, all of these terms describe the way that the colors in a skein array themselves in the knitted sock—generally in a way the knitter finds undesirable or unattractive.

If this has ever happened to you, and you didn't know how to change or stop these effects, then read on. There are ways that you can avoid splotching, pooling, stacking, striping, and other similar effects. It all has to do with the yarn's repeat.

The simplest way to understand a "repeat" is to think about the dyeing process. When hand-dyers are preparing to dye yarn, the first thing they do is wind the yarn into a hank, an oblong coil of parallel loops of yarn, secured in at least two places by ties. (There is some debate over whether a long coil of yarn like this is called a "hank" or a "skein" or both; for convenience, I've called it a "hank.") Hanks can vary in length depending on the kind of equipment the dyer uses, but the circumference of a hank generally ranges from 36 to 72 inches (one to two meters). That means that the length of each parallel loop of yarn that makes up the hank is 36 to 72 inches, and the dyer has a 36- to 72-inch "palette" of loops on which to apply the dye.

The dyer stretches out the hank on a table or workspace, smoothing out the strands, to have access to all of the strands that make up the hank of yarn. Whether the color is applied by brushing, or pouring, or squirting, or some other method, the multicolored effect is created applying color to one segment of the loop, then applying another color to the next segment, and so on, until the entire hank is finished. Thus, the length of each section of color may vary.

When the yarn is dry and wound in a ball and you start to knit with it, you begin to work your way though the color segments. The colors that the dyer has applied show up in the rows of knitted stitches. You may not have ever stopped to think about the order in which those colors appear as you knit them; you may have just enjoyed the rapid change of colors as they fly beneath your needles. But if you stop and look at the order in which you come to the colors, you'll see that they form a fairly regular

The color in these socks pools and flashes.

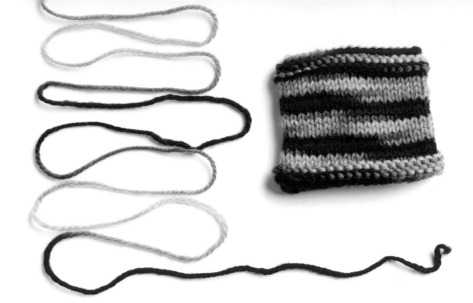

Examining a length of yarn lets you see the repeat clearly.

sequence created by the order in which the colors were applied to the individual strands; this is the repeat.

Let's take a look at a specific yarn so you can see how this works. Above is a brightly colored swatch and the yarn it was knitted from. When you look at the swatch, at first all you can see is a riot of color, but stretch out a strand of the yarn and compare it to the knitted fabric, and you can start to see the orderly sequence of colors that make up this yarn's repeat. The first portion of the yarn is an eleven-inch segment of red. After about four inches of orange, the next color is yellow. After the yellow comes green, then blue, then a long stretch of purple. Then the colors reverse until they're back at red. So the color repeat of this skein of yarn is: Red, orange, yellow, green, blue, purple, blue, green, yellow, orange, red. That particular pattern of colors will repeat itself over and over again as you continue to knit the strands of yarn.

If you go back and look at the hank of yarn before it is wound into a ball (see far right), you can see this sequence of colors very easily. Pick a starting point and follow the sequence of colors around the hank of yarn. Yep, there it is again: red to purple and back again, over and over again as you follow the yarn all the way through the hank.

Now that you know what a repeat is, you'll be able to find it on nearly any hank of multicolored yarn. If the yarn has not been rewound since it was dyed, you can simply untwist the hank and carefully lay out the hank so you can see the order in which the dye was applied.

✤ RESKEINING

Why do hand-dyers go to the trouble of reskeining their yarn before displaying and selling it? Many people feel that a skein of yarn that hasn't been rewound simply doesn't look as pretty as a skein of yarn that has—and as a result it may not sell as well. Customers may also have a hard time envisioning how the disparate segments of color in a hank will look when they are actually knit up; by rewinding the yarn, the dyer shuffles up the color segments to give a better idea of how the colors work together.

A hank of yarn may be rewound to be longer or shorter after it is dyed.

Often, however, handpainted yarns will not still be in the original hank that the dyer used—they've been reskeined into a different-sized hank. (You'll know a hank of yarn has been reskeined if the colors are already mixed up randomly in the hank rather than lining up neatly in rows.) If this is the case, you'll need to stretch out the end of the yarn, being very careful not to tangle the remainder of the hank, and look for the repeat on that strand. Once you examine the individual strand of yarn, you'll be able to figure out the sequence of color segments and thus figure out the repeat.

Why Yarn Pools

When you knit a sock, you are creating a seamless tube. You start at one end— say, the cuff—and work your way down the leg. As you knit, you are taking the yarn around and around in a circular path. Think of the cardboard tube from a roll of paper towels; if you pull it off the holder and it comes apart at the seams, you'll see the cardboard spiral around, taking the same path that your sock yarn does when you're knitting along.

As you work around in this spiral path, the yarn ends up stacking up in rows, one on top of another. The colors progress on this spiral path in the order of the color repeat. The color pattern will repeat itself over and over again, around and around the tube, as you knit your sock.

This, my friends, is why you have pooling. As the color repeat winds its way around and around the knitted tube, segments of color end up sitting next to each other or on top of each other. When one color in one row sits up against the same color in the next row, and the next and maybe the next, it can create a massing of that one color that draws the eye.

Pooling has an element of randomness to it: you never know exactly what it will look like until you knit with the yarn. Sometimes pooling creates semi-regular patterns like zigzags or swirls. Sometimes the yarn is almost but not quite the right size to stripe, creating swags of almost-stripes. Sometimes the pooling ends up just looking like big blotches of color. Every once in a while, fate intervenes, and you'll see some incredible pattern that looks like argyle diamonds or a trellis or something equally symmetrical (so long as you keep knitting along in the same-sized tube).

Rewinding a hank shows how the colors work together.

A yarn with short color segments knits up in a sock with no pooling.

If you like the way in which your yarn is pooling, then that's easy enough: just keep doing what you're doing. But if you don't like the effect you're getting, then read on to learn how to change it—or how to select yarns that are less likely to pool.

Look to the Length

The critical factor in whether a yarn will pool (and how pronounced the pooling will be) is the length of each color segment in the yarn. We've already talked about how to determine the repeat of a particular skein of sock yarn by looking at the order of the color segments as they appear on the strand of yarn. But it's at least as important to consider the length of each color segment in the repeat. Simply put, the shorter the color segments, the less pooling you will have. The longer the color segments, the more pooling you will have, and the more dramatic the pooling will be.

Don't believe it's that simple? Here are a few examples that will convince you. The yarn on the left was dyed using very small, narrow color segments. In the strand of yarn next to the sock, you can see that no individual segment is longer than two or three inches, and some are even shorter than that. Now see how the yarn looks when knit into an average-sized sock cuff; the small segments of color get shuffled around the circumference of the tube. They aren't long enough to extend from row to row, so they don't make swags or swooshes or zigzags. The color segments are distributed throughout the yarn and line up randomly from row to row, so they don't tend to form masses of color that look like splotches.

Above right is an example of the exact opposite: this yarn was dyed with color segments that are several inches long. The long color segments mean that the same color extends over many stitches and sometimes carries over into more than one round. Because the areas of each color are longer, they are more likely to stack up on top of each other, creating blotching, semi-striping, and other effects. Sure enough, take a look at the same yarn when knit into a sock cuff. Yep, there's the pooling as the lo-o-o-ong color segments stack on top of each other and make zigzags.

Here's something to remember, however: if each color segment is long enough to extend all the way around the circumference of the sock one or more times, i.e., if you can knit one or more complete rounds without there being a change in color (like the pink yarn to the right), you will get stripes. How thick the stripes are depends largely on how long the color segments are. This is the genius behind deliberately self-striping yarns, whether sock yarns (like the Regia Nation and Crazy Colors series) or thicker yarns (Nashua Wooly Stripes and Noro Kureyon, for example). The next time you're knitting with a self-striping yarn, notice the length of the color repeats. You'll find that they are very, very long, sometimes measuring in feet or yards rather than inches.

From the sock knitter's perspective, however, the dicey part comes when the color segments are intermediate in length. They are just a bit too long to be distributed randomly across the rows but not quite long enough to create manageable stripes. Here is where you will have the most uncertainty and where you will have to do the most playing around (and, unfortunately, ripping out). If a yarn has even one intermediate-length color segment in its repeat, it's very likely to pool.

Pooling Be Gone!

Now that you understand how pooling comes about, what can you do about it? I mean, you can't change the yarn, right? And what if it turns out that lots and lots of sock yarn in your stash seems likely to pool? You aren't morally obligated to buy more yarn (sorry!); you just need to make the most of the stuff you have.

Begin by knowing yourself. If you don't care very much about pooling, if the color effects don't bug you but rather fascinate you, then just knit happily away and admire the patterns that your yarn creates. On the other hand, if pooling drives you crazy and you absolutely hate the way it looks, then start taking a good, hard look at each skein of sock yarn *before* you buy it. Stretch out a strand of the yarn carefully (if you have to fiddle with a skein, courtesy requires that you ask the vendor if it's okay). Figure out the color repeat, and then get a feel for how long each individual segment of color is. If each color segment is an inch or less in length, and you're knitting about 7 to 8 stitches per inch on an average-sized sock, you should have minimal pooling. If the lengths of individual color are longer than, say, forty or fifty inches, you'll probably get distinct stripes that occur in a regular pattern. If the color segments are just a little shy of this number, you may end up with near-stripes of nearly one or two full rows, creating a kind of zigzagged striping effect. And if the lengths fall some-

This yarn was dyed to produce stripes in two shades of pink.

where in between, you'll have to prepare yourself for the possibility of pooling or splotching, knowing that the longer the repeats, the more obvious the pooling will be.

Great, you say, but I already have a bunch of yarns in my stash that look like they are likely to pool. How can I know for sure what the pooling will look like?

Aw, c'mon, you know what I'm going to say, don't you? The only way to know for sure how a yarn will pool is to knit it up.

①

The top and bottom are started from a different point on the repeat.

③

A small change in gauge can mean a big change in pooling.

②

Four extra stitches in the foot of this sock make pooling much more pronounced

Working Around Pooling

Suppose you cast on a pair of socks using a gorgeous new handpainted yarn you just bought at a fiber festival. You've knitted a few inches of the cuff when all of a sudden you get that sinking feeling in your stomach. You can see the yarn start to pool, and you don't like the way it looks. Is there no hope?

Before you panic and use that yarn to tie up your tomatoes, take a deep breath and try one of the following strategies.

1 Try casting on again, but start at a different place in the repeat. It sounds silly—you're using the same yarn, the same needles, the same number of stitches— but beginning at a different point in the color repeat can dramatically alter the way the yarn pools (or doesn't pool).

2 Change your gauge. Even a difference of a half-stitch per inch can sometimes be enough to change the stacking of the yarn and minimize or avoid pooling. So try going up or down a needle size (or a fraction of a size, if you use the metric system).

3 Change the number of stitches per round. More or fewer stitches per round may shake up the way the colors stack, leaving you satisfied with the end result instead of angst-ridden.

4

The top half, worked in seed stitch, doesn't stripe like the bottom half, in stockinette.

5

The top half, worked with two alternating balls of yarn, has more blended color than the bottom half.

4 Try a different pattern or stitch. Different stitches and different patterns use up different amounts of yarn per row. For example, you may have heard the general rule that stitches with yarnovers tend to use less yarn per row than solid stockinette. Conversely, a pattern stitch that involves frequently moving the working yarn from front to back and vice versa, like seed stitch, tends to use up more yarn per row than plain stockinette. A change in pattern or stitch may do the trick.

5 Try alternating balls of yarn within the same sock. Knit one or two rows with the first ball, then knit the next one or two rows with the other. Other than making sure you twist the yarns when you switch from one ball to the next, this is a pretty easy and almost foolproof way to mix up the colors and eliminate pooling and splotching. Just make sure that each ball begins at a different place in the repeat (i.e., start with a different colored segment) when you start knitting.

Make sure you pay attention to any resulting change in gauge. Changing needle size or the number of cast-on stitches will also change the size of the finished sock.

Why do these tricks work? Well, as you well know, there isn't anything a knitter can do to change the length of the individual color segments in a given ball of yarn. But you can change some of the other variables that affect pooling: starting at a different point in the yarn will change the order in which the color segments play out, possibly minimizing pooling; changing the size of the tube you're knitting (by changing the number of cast-on stitches or needle size) will alter how the colors stack up on each other; and changing the rate at which the yarn is used up in a round will also make the colors stack up differently, creating different color patterns.

Still no joy with that particularly stubborn pooler? Don't fret: if you've got a handpainted yarn that's an intransigent pooler, look no further than the pattern section of this book. The Spread Spectrum Socks, for example, use multidirectional knitting to see pooling in a new way, and the Corrugated Socks use vertical rows with stranded knitting to break up any pooling effects.

Before you turn to the pattern section, let me remind you of one more thing: there's just no substitute for getting the yarn on the needles and testing it out. You can study color segments all you want, you can fiddle with gauge and play around with stitch patterns, but the only definite way to know what will happen when you knit a particular skein of yarn into a specific sock pattern is to do it. Don't be afraid to experiment, even if it means ripping out what you've been working on. It's much better to rip out a few inches of a sock and start again, ultimately ending up with a pair of socks you finish and love, than to slog along with a sock that just isn't pleasing you, a sock that will sit, abandoned and unfinished, at the bottom of your knitting bag.

Patterns
for Handpainted Yarns

The following twenty-one patterns were designed especially to show off your treasured skeins of handpainted yarn to their best advantage (though many of them will look great even in solid yarns—go on, break all the rules!).

Look for these symbols, which are my suggestions for pairing yarn and pattern:

Nearly Solid

Muted Multi

Wild Multi

Longbourn Socks

Kristi Schueler

These socks were inspired by the wallpaper in the dining room of Longbourn, the Bennets' house, in the BBC production of *Pride and Prejudice*. This tessellated pattern works best when there is a value contrast between the solid and multicolored yarns. The lazy daisy embroidery on the cuff not only adds a feminine touch but also helps tack down long floats inside the sock.

FINISHED SIZE
About 7½ (9)" (19 [23] cm) foot circumference and 8½ (9½)" (21.5 [24] cm) long from back of heel to tip of toe.

YARN
Fingering weight (#1 Super Fine).
Shown here: Araucania Ranco Solid (75% wool, 25% nylon; 376 yd [344 m]/100 g): #106 semi-solid denim (blue), 1 skein. CC: Araucania Ranco Multi (75% wool, 25% nylon; 376 yd [344 m]/100 g): #303 pink/coral/lavender, 1 skein.

NEEDLES
Inner picot edge—Size 1 (2.5 mm): set of 4 double-pointed (dpn). Outer picot edge and remaining sock—Size 2 (2.75 mm): set of 4 dpn. Adjust needle size if necessary to obtain the correct gauge.

NOTIONS
Marker (m); tapestry needle.

GAUGE
16 stitches and 17 rounds = 2" (5 cm) in stockinette stitch worked in the round on smaller needles.

Longbourn Leg Chart

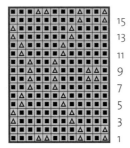

15
13
11
9
7
5
3
1

Longbourn Instep Chart

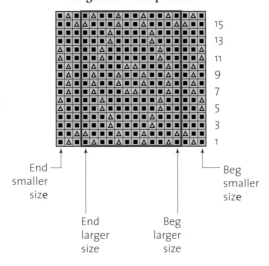

15
13
11
9
7
5
3
1

End smaller size

Beg smaller size

End larger size

Beg larger size

Checkerboard Chart

1

■ with A, knit
▲ with B, knit
□ pattern repeat

Leg

With smaller needles and B, loosely CO 60 (72) sts. Divide sts evenly on 3 dpns [20 (24) sts on each needle], place marker (pm), and join for working in the rnd, being careful not to twist sts. Rnd begins at back of leg.

Knit 6 rnds. Change to larger needles and knit 1 rnd.

Next rnd: *K2tog, yo; repeat from * to end.

Knit 7 more rounds.

Next rnd: *Pick up first CO edge st and knit together with next st on left needle; rep from * to end.

Attach A and work Longbourn Leg Chart 3 times, or until desired length of leg to top of heel, ending after Rnd 16 of chart.

Heel

With B only and Needle 1, k16 (19), work short-rows (see Glossary, page 123). Slip rem sts from Needle 1 to Needle 2. With WS facing, sl 1 purlwise (pwise) with yarn in front (wyf), p27 (33) sts onto Needle 1, wrap and turn (w & t), slip any remaining sts from Needle 3 to Needle 2—30 (36) heel sts on Needle 1 centered at back of leg with one wrapped stitch at each end. Rem 30 (36) sts on Needle 2 will be worked later for instep.

First Half

Work 30 (36) heel sts back and forth in rows on Needle 1 as foll:

Row 1: (RS) Sl 1 pwise with yarn in back (wyb), knit to last st before wrapped st, w & t.

Row 2: Sl 1 pwise wyf, purl to last st before wrapped st, w & t.

Rep Rows 1 and 2 eight (ten) more times—10 (12) wrapped sts on each side; 10 (12) unwrapped sts in center.

Second Half

Row 1: (RS) Sl 1 pwise wyb, knit to first wrapped st, work wrap(s) tog with st, w & t [one st double wrapped].

Row 2: Sl 1 pwise wyf, purl to first wrapped st, work wrap(s) tog with st, w & t [2 sts double wrapped; one at each end].

Rep Rows 1 and 2 eight (ten) more times—1 wrapped st remains on each side. Resume working in the round as foll:

Next rnd: On Needle 1, knit to rem wrapped st, work wrap tog with st through back loop (tbl); on Needle 2, reattach A and work 30 (36) sts in Longbourn Instep Chart (beg and end where indicated on chart for your size); with Needle 3, work wrap tog with st tbl, work 15 (18) stitches in Checkerboard Chart.

Foot

Cont even, working Checkerboard Chart on Needles 1 and 3 for sole and Longbourn Instep Chart on Needle 2 for instep, until piece measures about 6 (7)" (16.5 [18] cm) from back of heel, or about 2 (2½)" (5 [6] cm) less than desired total foot length.

Toe

Work in St st with B as foll:

Rnd 1: On Needle 1, knit to last 3 sts, k2tog, k1; on Needle 2, k1, ssk, knit to last 3 sts, k2tog, k1; on Needle 3, k1, ssk, knit to end—4 sts dec'd.

Rnd 2: Knit.

Rep Rnds 1 and 2 six (eight) more times—32 (36) sts rem. Rep Rnd 1 every rnd five (six) times—12 sts rem. Knit the sts on Needle 1 onto the end of Needle 3—6 sts each on 2 needles.

Finishing

Cut yarn, leaving a 12" (30.5 cm) tail. Thread tail on a tapestry needle and use the Kitchener st (see Glossary, page 120) to graft sts tog. Weave in loose ends. Block lightly.

Thread 1 (2) yd (1.5 [2] m) of B on a tapestry needle. Embroider a lazy daisy (see Glossary, page 120) centered over each full square around the circumference of the sock.

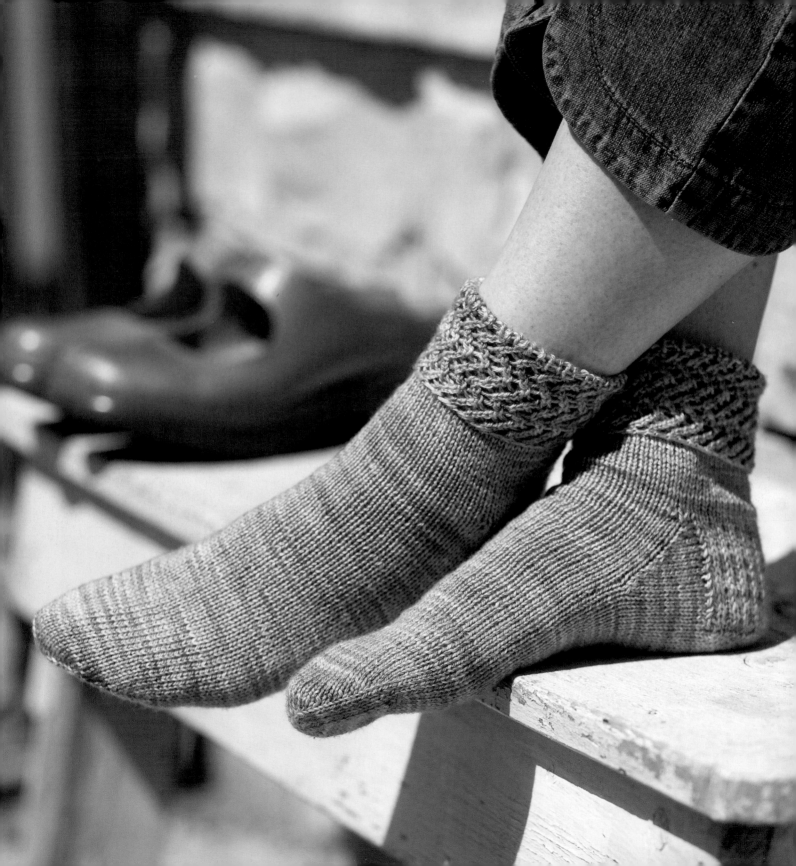

Zigzag Anklets

Pam Grushkin

Handpainted sock yarn has traditionally been made from wool, but new fibers like bamboo, Tencel, and soy are revolutionizing the options available to the sock knitter. These cuffed socks show off the sheen of a merino/Tencel blend, and the shorter style and cooler fiber blend make these the perfect option for warm weather.

FINISHED SIZE
Sock measures about 6¼ (7, 7½, 8)" (16 [18, 19, 20.5] cm) foot circumference and about 8½ (9, 9½, 10)" (21.5 [23, 24, 25.5] cm) from back of heel to tip of toe.

YARN
Fingering weight (#1 Super Fine).
Shown here: Blue Moon Seduction (50% merino wool, 50% Tencel; 400 yd [366 m]/ 113 g): algae, 1 skein.

NEEDLES
Lace cuff—U.S. size 1 (2.25 mm): set of 4 double-pointed (dpn). Stockinette section—U.S. size 3 (2.75 mm): set of 4 double-pointed (dpn). Adjust needle size if necessary to obtain the correct gauge.

NOTIONS
Markers (m); tapestry needle.

GAUGE
16 stitches and 22 rounds = 2" (5 cm) in stockinette stitch worked in the round on larger needles; 12 stitches and 28 rounds = 2" (5 cm) in patt worked in the round on smaller needles.

Zigzag Pattern

(mult of 2 sts)

Rnd 1 and all odd-numbered rnds: Knit
Rnds 2, 4, and 6: *Yo, k2tog; rep from * to end.
Rnds 8, 10, and 12: *Ssk, yo; rep from * to end.
Rep Rnds 1–12 for Zigzag Patt.

Zigzag Chart

	knit
⊙	yo
⊠	k2tog
⊠	ssk
	pattern repeat

Cuff

With larger needles and using the long-tail method (see Glossary, page 119), loosely CO 40 (46, 50, 54) sts. Arrange sts as evenly as possible on 3 dpn and place marker (pm).

Position needles so that the last CO st (on the right-hand needle) and the first CO st (on the left-hand needle) are next to each other. Being careful not to twist sts, sl first st on left-hand needle to the right-hand needle. Sl second st on right-hand needle (the last CO st) to the left-hand needle. This reduces the gap at the join.

Change to smaller needles and work Zigzag patt 2 times, ending after Rnd 12—piece measures about 1¾" (4.5 cm) from CO.

Next rnd: (fold line) Knit and at the same time inc 10 sts evenly as you go—50 (56, 60, 64) sts.

Work k1, p1 rib for 1½" (3.8 cm).

Turn sock inside out so that RS of Zigzag patt folds over ribbing. The needle with the working yarn will be in your left hand. To begin to work in St st in the opposite direction, sl st below first st on right-hand needle onto left-hand needle and knit it tog with first st on left-hand needle.

Change to larger needles and work in St st until piece measures 3½" (9 cm) from fold line.

Heel

Heel Flap

Rearrange sts so that there are 24 (28, 30, 32) sts on Needle 1; rem 26 (28, 30, 32) will be worked later for instep. Work heel sts back and forth in rows as foll:

Row 1: (RS) *Sl 1 purlwise (pwise) with yarn in back (wyb), k1; repeat from * to end.
Row 2: (WS) Sl 1 pwise with yarn in front (wyf), purl to end.
Rep Rows 1 and 2 eleven (thirteen, fourteen, fifteen) more times—12 (14, 15, 16) chain sts along each selvedge edge; heel flap measures about 2¼ (2½, 2¾, 3)" (5 cm).

Turn Heel

Work short-rows (see Glossary, page 123) to shape heel as foll:

Row 1: (RS) Sl 1 pwise wyb, k13 (15, 16, 17), ssk, k1, turn work.
Row 2: Sl 1 pwise wyf, p5, p2tog, p1, turn.
Row 3: Sl 1 pwise wyb, knit last st before gap formed on prev row, ssk (1 st from each side of gap), k1, turn.
Row 4: Sl 1 pwise wyf, purl to last st before gap formed on prev row, p2tog (1 st from each side of gap), p1, turn.
Rep Rows 3 and 4 until all heel sts have been worked—14 (16, 18, 18) sts rem on Needle 1. On the last 2 rows, omit the k1 or p1 after dec if necessary.

Shape Gussets

Pick up sts along selvedge edges of heel flap and rejoin for working in the rnd as foll:

Rnd 1: With Needle 1, k14 (16, 18, 18) heel sts, then pick up and knit (see Glossary, page 122) 12 (14, 15, 16) sts along edge of heel flap (picking up in both halves of each chain st); with Needle 2, pick up and knit 1 st bet heel and instep, and knit it tog with first instep st, k24 (26, 28, 30) instep sts, then pick up and knit 1 st bet heel and instep and knit it tog with last instep st; with Needle 3, pick up and knit 12 (14, 15, 16) sts along other edge of

heel flap (picking up in both halves of each chain st), then knit across 7 (8, 9, 9) heel sts —64 (72, 78, 82) sts total; 19 (22, 24, 25) sts each Needles 1 and 3, 26 (28, 30, 32) sts on Needle 2. Place marker (pm) for beg of rnd. Rnd begins at back of heel.

Rnd 2: Knit.

Rnd 3: On Needle 1, knit to last three sts, ssk, k1; on Needle 2, knit; on Needle 3, k1, k2tog, knit to end—2 sts dec'd. Rep Rnds 2 and 3 six (seven, eight, eight) more times—50 (56, 60, 64) sts rem.

Foot

Work even in St st until sock measures 7¼ (7½, 7¾, 8)" (18.5 [19, 19.5, 20.5] cm) or 1¼ (1½, 1¾, 2)" (3.2 [3.8, 4.5, 5] cm) less than desired length from back of heel to tip of toe.

Toe Shaping

Rnd 1: On Needle 1, knit to last 3 sts, k2tog, k1; on Needle 2, k1, ssk, knit to last 3 sts, k2tog, k1; on Needle 3, k1, ssk, knit to end of rnd—4 sts dec'd.

Rnd 2: Knit.

Rep Rnds 1 and 2 five (six, seven, seven) more times—26 (28, 28, 32) sts rem. Then rep Rnd 1 four times—10 (12, 12, 16) sts remain.

With Needle 3, knit across sts on Needle 1—5 (6, 6, 8) sts on each Needle.

Finishing

Arrange sts evenly on 2 dpns. Cut yarn, leaving a 14" (35.5 cm) tail. With tail threaded on tapestry needle, use the Kitchener st (see Glossary, page 120) to graft rem sts. Weave in ends. Block lightly.

Punctuated Rib Socks

Ann Budd

These socks are worked from the toe up, beginning with the Eastern cast-on and ending with a sewn bind-off. To interrupt potential color pooling, the leg and instep are worked in a modified k4, p1 rib pattern punctuated with horizontal two- and four-stitch floats.

FINISHED SIZE
About 6½ (7¼)" (16.5 [18.5] cm) foot circumference, 8¾ (10¼)" (22 [26] cm) foot length from back of heel to tip of toe, and 7 (8¼)" (18 [21] cm) leg length from top of sock to base of foot.

YARN
Fingering weight (#1 Super Fine).
Shown here: Black Bunny Fibers Superwash Merino Sock (100% wool; 400 yd [366 m]/4 oz): Marie Antoinette, 1 skein.

NEEDLES
Foot and lower leg—U.S. size 1 (2.25 mm): set of 4 double-pointed (dpn). Upper leg—U.S. size 2 (2.75 mm): set of 4 dpn. Adjust needle size if necessary

to obtain the correct gauge.

NOTIONS
Markers (m); tapestry needle.

GAUGE
16 sts and 24 rows = 2" (5 cm) in stockinette stitch worked in the round.

NOTE
Because the stitch pattern repeats over a relatively large number of stitches, only two sizes are provided. To make a slightly smaller or larger sock than given, use needles one or two sizes smaller or larger (but understand that the knitted fabric will be slightly tighter or looser if you do so) and adjust the length of the foot as necessary.

 STITCH GUIDE

Wrapped Rib Pattern
(mult of 10 sts)

Rnd 1: *P1, k1 tbl, k2, k1 tbl; rep from *.

Rnd 2 and all even-numbered rnds: Rep Rnd 1.

Rnd 3: *P1, k1 tbl, insert right-hand needle between 2nd and 3rd sts on left-hand needle, draw up a loop, place it on left-hand needle, then knit it tog with the first st on left-hand needle, k1, k1 tbl, p1, k1 tbl, k2, k1 tbl; rep from *.

Rnd 5: *P1, insert right-hand needle between 4th and 5th sts on left-hand needle, draw up a loop, place it on left-hand needle, then knit it tog with the first st on left-hand needle, k2, k1 tbl, p1, k1 tbl, k2, k1 tbl.

Rnd 7: Rep Rnd 3.

Rnd 9: Rep Rnd 1.

Rnd 11: *P1, k1 tbl, k2, k1 tbl, p1, k1 tbl, insert right-hand needle between 2nd and 3rd sts on left needle, draw up a loop, place it on left-hand needle, then knit it tog with the first st on left-hand needle, k1, k1 tbl; rep from *.

Rnd 13: *P1, k1 tbl, k2, k1 tbl, p1, insert right-hand needle between 4th and 5th sts on left-hand needle, draw up a loop, place it on left-hand needle, then knit it tog with the first st on left-hand needle, k2, k1 tbl; rep from *.

Rnd 15: Rep Rnd 11.

Rnd 16: Rep Rnd 1.

Rep Rnds 1–16 for Wrapped Rib patt.

Cuff Wrapped Rib Pattern
(mult of 5 sts)

Rnd 1: *P1, k1 tbl, insert right-hand needle between 2nd and 3rd sts on left-hand needle, draw up a loop, place it on left-hand needle, then knit it tog with the first st on left-hand needle, k1, k1 tbl; rep from * around.

Rnd 2 and all even-numbered rnds: *P1, k1 tbl, k2, k1 tbl; rep from *.

Rnd 3: *P1, insert right-hand needle between 4th and 5th sts on left-hand needle, draw up a loop, place it on left-hand needle, then knit it tog with the first st on left-hand needle, k2, k1 tbl; rep from * around.

Rnd 5: Rep Rnd 1.

Rnd 6: Rep Rnd 2.

Wrapped Rib Chart

15
13
11
9
7
5
3
1

Cuff Wrapped Rib Chart

5
3
1

☐ knit

• purl

ℚ k1 tbl

⇨ Insert right-hand needle between 2nd and 3rd sts, draw up a loop, place it on left-hand needle, then knit it tog with first st on left-hand needle, k1.

⇨ Insert right-hand needle between 4th and 5th sts, draw up a loop, place it on left-hand needle, then knit it tog with first st on left-hand needle, k2, k1 tbl.

☐ pattern repeat

Toe

With smaller needles and using the Eastern method (see Glossary, page 119), cast on 8 (12) sts (4 [6] sts each on 2 needles). With a third needle, knit the first 2 (3) sts on the first needle again. There are now 2 (3) bottom-of-foot sts on Needle 1; 4 (6) top-of-foot sts on Needle 2; and 2 (3) bottom-of-foot sts on Needle 3. The rnd begins at the center of the bottom of the foot, between Needle 1 and Needle 3. Using the M1 method (see Glossary, page 121), inc 1 st at each edge of bottom-of-foot sts and top-of-foot sts as foll:

Rnd 1: On Needle 1, K2, M1, k1; on Needle 2, k1, M1, k4, M1, k1; on Needle 3, k1, M1, k2—4 sts inc'd; 12 (16) sts total.

Rnd 2: On Needle 1, Knit to last st, M1, k1; on Needle 2, K1, M1, knit to last st, M1, k1; on Needle 3, k1, M1, knit to last st—4 sts inc'd.

Rep Rnd 2 three (four) more times—28 (36) sts total; 7 (9) sts on Needle 1, 14 (18) sts on Needle 2, 7 (9) sts on Needle 3.

Rnd 3: Knit.

Rep Rnds 2 and 3 (i.e., increase every other rnd) 8 times—60 (68) sts total; 15 (17) sts on Needle 1, 30 (34) sts on Needle 2, 15 (17) sts on Needle 3.

Size 6¹/₂" only

Rearrange sts so there are 14 sts on Needle 1, 32 sts on Needle 2, and 14 sts on Needle 3.

Foot

Set-up rnd: On Needle 1, knit; on Needle 2, k1 (2), work Rnd 1 of Wrapped Rib patt 3 times, p1, k0 (1); on Needle 3, Knit. Cont in patt as established until piece measures 7 (8)" (18 [20.5] cm) from CO, or about 1¾ (2¼)" (4.5 [5.5] cm) less than desired total foot length, ending between Needle 2 and Needle 3 (i.e., do not work the sts on Needle 3). Make note of last rnd of chart worked so second sock can be made to match.

Heel

Sl sts from Needle 1 to Needle 3; then sl 15 (17) sts from Needle 2 to empty Needle 1—30 (34) heel (bottom-of-foot) sts are on Needle 3; 30 (34) instep (top-of-foot) sts are divided between Needles 1 and 2. On Needle 3, work the 30 (34) heel sts back and forth in short-rows in two parts as foll:

First Half

In the first half, one fewer st is worked every row so that the sts in the center of needle are worked for the greatest number of rows, creating the fabric pouch at the center of the heel.

Row 1: (RS) Knit to last st (do not work last st), turn work.

Row 2: (WS) Yo backward (i.e., bring yarn from back to front; see Glossary, page 121), purl to last st (do not work last st), turn. The yo will make a paired st with the first st knitted. (Working the yo backward creates a tighter st.)

Row 3: Yo as usual (i.e., bring yarn from front to back), knit to paired sts at end of needle (do not work paired sts), turn.

Row 4: Yo backward, purl to paired sts at end of needle (do not work paired sts), turn.

Rep Row 3 and 4 until 12 (14) single sts rem between paired sts (14 [16] sts between yarnovers), ending having worked to the paired sts at the end of a RS (knit) row. Do not turn the work.

Second Half

In the second half, one more st is worked every row so that the sts at the sides are gradually worked back in. With the RS still facing, continue with the last row of the first half as foll:

Row 1: (RS) K1 (the first st of the paired sts), correct the mount of the yo so that the leading edge of the yo is on the front of the needle, k2tog (the yo with the first st of the next pair), leaving a yo as the first st on the left needle. Turn.

Row 2: (WS) Yo backward, purl to first set of paired sts, purl the first st of the pair, ssp (the yo with the first st of the next pair; see Glossary, page 120), leaving a yo as the first st on the left needle. Turn.

Row 3: Yo as usual, knit to the first paired st, knit the first st of the pair (the next 2 sts will be yarnovers), correct the mount of the 2 yarnovers, k3tog (the 2 yarnovers with the first st of the next pair), turn.

Row 4: Yo backward, purl to the first paired st, purl the first st of the pair (the next 2 sts will be yarnovers), sssp (the 2 yarnovers with the first st of the next pair; see Glossary, page 120), turn.

Rep Rows 3 and 4 until all the yarnovers of the first half have been worked, ending with Row 4. The last turn will bring the RS facing—there will be 1 yo at the end of the heel needle.

Rejoin for Working in Rounds

Size 6¹/₂" only

With RS facing, yo as usual, knit to the yo at the end of the heel sts, transfer this yo to the beginning of the instep sts and work it tog with the first instep st as k2tog, work to the last instep st in Wrapped Rib patt as established, work the last instep st tog with the yo at the beginning of the heel sts as ssk—60 sts.

Size 7¹/₄" only

With RS facing, yo as usual, knit to the yo at the end of the heel sts, pick up the horizontal bar as for M1 between the heel and instep sts and knit it tog with the yo as k2tog, work to the last instep st in patt as established, pick up the horizontal bar between the instep and heel sts and knit it tog as ssk—70 sts.

Leg

To prevent a ladder of loose sts from forming along the front of the leg, rearrange the sts so that 30 (35) instep sts are on Needle 2, 15 (17) heel sts are on Needle 3, and 15 (18) heel sts are on Needle 1. Cont in patt as estab-

lished (working Wrapped Rib patt on 31 instep sts and rem sts in St st) for 10 (14) rnds—piece measures about 3" (7.5 cm) from base of heel. Maintaining continuity of patt on instep, work Wrapped Rib patt across all sts until piece measures about 3½ (4)" (9 [10] cm) from base of heel. Change to larger needles and cont in patt until piece measures about 6½ (7¾)" (16.5 [19.5] cm) from base of heel, ending with Rnd 2 or 10 of Wrapped Rib patt. Work in Cuff Wrapped Rib patt for 6 rnds, ending with rnd 6 of Cuff Wrapped Rib patt.

Finishing

Cut yarn about 3 times the circumference of the leg. Thread yarn on a tapestry needle and use the sewn method (see Glossary, page 118) to bind off all sts. Weave in loose ends, tightening cast-on sts at toe if necessary. If necessary, tighten up any holes along heel short-row turns. Block lightly.

Staccato Socks

Véronik Avery

Handpainted wool is too precious to part with, but what to do with those tiny leftover balls? This pattern uses one full skein of yarn and only sixty yards each of three additional colors, creating staccato bursts of color. The toe-up design lets you use every yard of your stash of handpainted mini-skeins.

Finished Size
About 9" (23 cm) foot circumference and 9" (23 cm) long from back of heel to tip of toe.

Yarn
Fingering weight (Super Fine #1).
Shown here: Koigu Painter's Palette Premium Merino (100% merino wool; 229 yd [209 m]/50 g): P138 (taupe/blue; A), 1 skein; P314 (taupe/pink; B), P602 (fuchsia/orange; C), and P621 (red/copper; D), about 60 yd (55 m) each.

Needles
U.S. size 0 (2 mm): set of 5 double-pointed (dpn) plus one extra. Adjust needle size if necessary to obtain the correct gauge.

Notions
Small amount of contrasting waste yarn; tapestry needle.

Gauge
14 stitches and 22 rounds = 2" (5 cm) in stockinette stitch worked in the round.

STITCH GUIDE

Wave Pattern
(mult of 16 sts)

Rnd 1: Knit, working any yos through the back loop (tbl).

Rnd 2: K1, [k2tog] twice, [k1, yo] twice, k2, [yo, k1] twice, [ssk] twice, k1.

Rep Rnds 1 and 2 for pattern.

Staggered Stripe Pattern

Rnds 1–12: *Work 2 rnds B, work 2 rnds A; rep from * twice more.

Rnds 13–24: *Work 2 rnds D, work 2 rnds B; rep from * twice more.

Rnds 25–36: *Work 2 rnds C, work 2 rnds A; rep from * twice more.

Rnds 37–52: *Work 2 rnds C, work 2 rnds B; rep from * twice more.

Wave Chart

□ knit
☒ k2tog
☉ yarnover
☒ ssk
☒ k1 tbl
□ pattern repeat

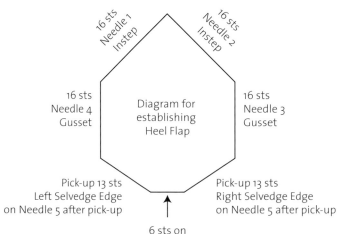

16 sts Needle 1 Instep

16 sts Needle 2 Instep

16 sts Needle 4 Gusset

16 sts Needle 3 Gusset

Diagram for establishing Heel Flap

Pick-up 13 sts Left Selvedge Edge on Needle 5 after pick-up

Pick-up 13 sts Right Selvedge Edge on Needle 5 after pick-up

6 sts on spare (6th) needle moved to Needle 5 during pick-ups

Toe

Using provisional method (see Glossary, page 119), waste yarn, and A, CO 16 sts. Divide evenly on 4 dpns—4 sts on each needle. Join for working in the round, being careful not to twist sts. Knit 1 rnd.

Next rnd: (inc rnd) On Needles 1 and 3, k1, make 1 (M1; see Glossary, page 121), knit to end; on Needles 2 and 4, knit to last st, M1, k1—4 sts inc'd.

Rep inc rnd 5 more times—40 sts, then alternate (inc 1 rnd, knit 1 rnd) 6 times—64 sts. Knit 4 rnds even.

Foot

On Needles 1 and 2, work Wave Chart; on Needles 3 and 4, knit; and at the same time work Staggered Stripe patt (see Stitch Guide) on all needles, until piece measures 6" (15 cm) or 3" (7.5 cm) less than desired finished foot length from CO, ending after Rnd 1 of Wave Chart.

Heel

Shape Gusset

Next rnd: (inc rnd) On Needles 1 and 2, work in patt as established; on Needle 3, M1, knit to end; on Needle 4, knit to end, M1—2 sts inc'd.

Next rnd: On Needles 1 and 2, work in patt as est, on Needles 3 and 4, knit.

Rep last 2 rnds 9 more times, working inc sts in St st as they become available—84 sts total; 16 sts on each Needle 1 and 2; 26 sts on each Needle 3 and 4. Do not break yarn.

Turn Heel

Sl last 10 sts of Needle 3 and first 10 sts of Needle 4 to spare needle (Needle 6). Join color A, and beg with a WS row and work back and forth in rows on 20 heel sts only.

Row 1: (WS) Work 1 row in St st on 6th dpn only.

Row 2: (RS; dec row) K1, k2tog, knit to last 3 sts, ssk, k1—2 sts dec'd.

Rep Rows 1 and 2 six more times—6 sts rem. Break yarn.

Heel Flap

With RS facing, empty needle (Needle 5) and A, pick up and knit (see Glossary, page 122) 13 sts along right selvedge of heel, k6 from 6th needle, then and pick up and knit 13 sts along left selvedge of heel—32 sts on Needle 5. Slip last st over next stitch on 4th needle—15 sts rem on Needle 4. Turn.

Row 1: (WS) Sl 1 purlwise (pwise) with yarn in front (wyf), purl to last st, p2tog (last st on Needle 5 and first st on Needle 3), turn—1 st dec'd.

Row 2: *Sl 1 pwise with yarn in back (wyb), k1; rep from * to last 2 sts, sl 1 pwise wyb, ssk (last st on Needle 5 and first st from Needle 4)—1 st dec'd.

Rep Rows 1 and 2 fourteen more times, then rep Row 1 once—32 sts on Needle 5; 0 sts rem on Needles 3 and 4. Break A and set aside 6th dpn.

Leg

Resume working in the round using yarn previously set aside as foll: on Needles 1 and 2, work in Wave patt as established; on Needle 5, work in Wave patt. Work until leg measures 2" (5 cm) from heel flap, ending on Row 2 of Wave patt. Change to A and purl 1 rnd, working any yos tbl. Break off other colors. Work in k2, p2 ribbing for 2¼" (5.5 cm). BO all sts.

Finishing

Remove waste yarn from CO and divide 16 revealed sts evenly on 2 needles (8 sts for top of toe, 8 sts for bottom of toe). Thread tail of CO yarn on a tapestry needle and use the Kitchener st (see Glossary, page 120) to graft toe sts tog. Weave in loose ends. Block lightly.

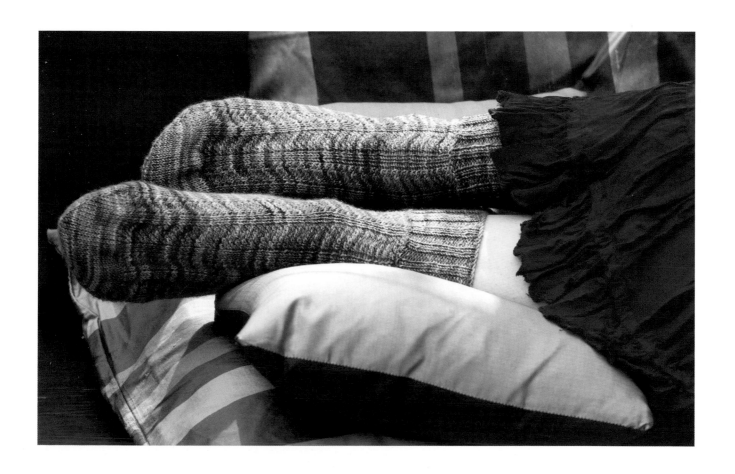

Copper Penny Socks

Nancy Bush

These socks began with part of a simple lace pattern from an Estonian knitting book, adding seed stitch columns between the lace pattern. The subtle color changes and closely related hues of the yarn add an extra dimension to the textured pattern. The half-handkerchief heel shaping echoes the small "V" shapes in the openwork pattern, while the French toe shaping is a vintage technique from *Weldon's Practical Needlework*.

FINISHED SIZE
About 7" (18 cm) foot circumference, 8" (20.5 cm) from top of cuff to to top of heel flap, and 9" (23 cm) from back of heel to tip of toe.

YARN
Fingering weight (Super Fine #1).
Shown here: Mountain Colors Bearfoot (60% superwash wool, 25% mohair, 15% nylon; 350 yd [320 m]/100 g): Red Tail Hawk, 1 skein.

NEEDLES
U.S. size 1 (2.25 mm): set of 5 double-pointed (dpn). Adjust needle size to obtain the correct gauge.

NOTIONS
Tapestry needle.

GAUGE
16 stitches and 19 rounds = 2" (5 cm) in stockinette stitch worked in the round.

STITCH GUIDE

Openwork Pattern
(mult of 9 sts)

Rnd 1: P1,*k1, yo, ssk, k1, k2tog, yo, k1, p2; rep from * to last 8 sts, k1, yo, ssk, k1, k2tog, yo, k1, p1.

Rnd 2: Knit.

Rnd 3: P1, *k2, yo, sl 1 knitwise (kwise) with yarn in back (wyb), k2tog, psso, yo, k2, p2; rep from * to last 8 sts, k2, yo, sl 1 kwise wyb, k2tog, psso, yo, k2, p1.

Rnd 4: Knit.

Ribbing Chart

3
1

☐ knit
• purl
⊙ yarn over
⊠ k2tog
⊠ ssk
☐ pattern repeat

Openwork Chart

3
1

Cuff

Using the double-start method (see Glossary, page 118) with the thumb yarn doubled, CO 54 sts over 2 dpns held tog. Arrange sts so that there are 13 sts on Needles 1 and 4 and 14 sts on Needles 2 and 3, place marker (pm), and join for working in the rnd, being careful not to twist sts. Rnd begins at back of leg. Knit 1 rnd, purl 1 rnd, and knit 1 rnd.

Leg

Work top ribbing as foll:

Rnd 1: P1, *k3, p1, k3, p2; rep from * to last 8 sts, k3, p1, k3, p1. Repeat Rnd 1 thirteen more times for cuff.

Work Openwork patt 18 times, ending after Rnd 4 of Openwork patt—piece measures about 8" (20.5 cm) from CO.

Heel

Heel Flap

Next Row: K13 sts from Needle 1, turn work. Sl 1, p25, turn—26 sts on Needle 1 for heel; 28 instep sts will be worked later.

Work 26 heel sts back and forth in rows as foll:

Row 1: (RS) *Sl 1 purlwise (pwise) wyb, k1; rep from * to end, turn.

Row 2: Sl 1 pwise with yarn in front (wyf), purl to end, turn.

Rep Rows 1 and 2 until 26 rows have been worked—13 chain edge sts at each selvedge.

Turn Heel

Work short-rows (see Glossary, page 123) to shape heel as foll:

Row 1: (RS) *K13, ssk, k1, turn—1 st dec'd.

Row 2: (WS) Sl 1 pwise wyf, p1, p2tog, p1, turn—1 st dec'd.

Row 3: Sl 1 pwise wyb, knit to last st before gap formed on prev row, ssk (1 st from each side of gap), k1, turn.

Row 4: Sl 1 pwise wyf, purl to last st before gap formed on prev row, p2tog (1 st from each side of gap), p1, turn.

Rep Rows 3 and 4 until all stitches are have been worked—14 heel sts rem.

Shape Gusset

Pick up sts along selvedge edges of heel flap and rejoin for working in the rnd as foll:

Rnd 1: With Needle 1, k14 heel sts, then pick up and knit 13 sts along edge of heel flap; with Needles 2 and 3, work across 28 instep sts as foll: k4, work Rnd 1 of Openwork patt as established across 20 sts; with Needle 4, pick up and knit 13 sts along other edge of heel flap, then k7 from heel needle—68 sts total; 20 sts each on Needles 1 and 4, 14 sts each on Needles 2 and 3. Rnd begins at beg of Needle 1.

Rnd 2: (dec rnd) On Needle 1, knit to last 3 sts, k2tog, k1; on Needles 2 and 3, work in patt as established; on Needle 4, k1, ssk, knit to end—2 sts dec'd.

Rnd 3: On Needle 1, knit; on Needles 2 and 3, work in patt as established; on Needle 4, knit.

Rep Rnds 2 and 3 six more times—54 sts rem; 13 sts each on Needles 1 and 4, 14 sts each on Needles 2 and 3.

Foot

Work in patt as established until foot measures 7" (18 cm) or 2" (5 cm) less than desired length from back of heel, ending with Rnd 4 of patt. Openwork patt should be worked about 30 times from CO edge. Knit 5 rnds.

Toe

Rearrange sts evenly over 3 needles as foll: sl first 5 sts from Needle 2 to end of Needle 1, sl last 5 sts on Needle 3 to beg of Needle 4, and move sts from Needle 2 to Needle 3—18 sts on each of 3 dpns. Rnd begins at bottom of foot.

Rnd 1: *K1, ssk, knit to last 3 sts on dpn, k2tog, k1; rep from * on each needle—6 sts dec'd.

Rnd 2: Knit.

Repeat Rnds 1 and 2 six more times—12 sts rem, 4 on each needle.

Next rnd: *K1, k2tog, k1; rep from * on each needle—9 sts rem, 3 sts on each needle.

Finishing

Cut yarn, leaving a 12" (30.5 cm) tail. Thread tail on tapestry needle, draw through rem sts, and pull snug to close the toe. Weave in loose ends. Block lightly.

Color Collision Socks

Chrissy Gardiner

These socks approach the problem of pooling sock yarn by rethinking the sock's structure: instead of the traditional vertical tube, they cleverly alternate flat garter-stitch strips with in-the-round ribbing. The frequent change in knitting direction sends the yarn's colors shooting every which way, ingeniously breaking up unattractive splotches. The unconventional structure also keeps these socks interesting to knit, even if you've made many pairs of socks before.

FINISHED SIZE
6 (7, 8)" (15 [18, 20.5] cm) foot circumference; 7½ (8½, 9½)" (19 [21.5, 24] cm) foot length from back of heel to tip of toe.

YARN
Fingering weight (Super Fine #1).
Shown here: Classic Elite Alpaca Sox (60% alpaca, 20% merino wool, 20% nylon; 450 yd [412 m]/100 g): color #1805, 1 skein.

NEEDLES
U.S. size 1 (2.25 mm): set of 5 double-pointed (dpn). Adjust needle size if necessary to obtain correct gauge.

GAUGE
17 stitches and 24 rounds = 2" (5 cm) in stockinette stitch worked in the round.

NOTIONS
Tapestry needle.

NOTE
If garter stitch bands are too loose compared to the ribbed rounds, work the garter stitch portions with smaller needles. If the ribbed rounds are too tight but the garter bands fit, work the ribbed rounds with larger needles. The garter stitch bands will be wider than the ribbed portions when the sock is not stretched. Try the socks on to check fit.

Cuff

First Garter Section

With one dpn, CO 14 sts. Work in garter stitch (knit every st on every row) for 96 (112, 128) rows. BO all sts and break yarn, leaving 12" (30.5 cm) tail. With tail threaded on tapestry needle, use invisible horizontal seam (see Glossary, page 122) to sew BO and CO edges together to form a tube.

First Ribbed Section

Pick up and knit (see Glossary, page 122) 48 (56, 64) sts along edge of garter tube (one st in each garter ridge). Arrange sts them evenly over across four dpns—12 (14, 16) sts on each needle. Join for working in the rnd. Work k1, p1 rib for about 1" (2.5 cm).

Second Garter Section

Using the backward loop method (see Glossary, page 118), CO 14 sts on end of needle just worked—26 (28, 30) sts on this needle. Turn.

Next row: K13, ssk (working last CO st together with first stitch of sock cuff), turn.

Next row: Sl 1 purlwise (pwise) with yarn in back (wyb), knit to end.

Rep last 2 rnds 47 (55, 63) more times—96 (112, 128) rows.

BO all sts and cut yarn, leaving a 12" (30.5 cm) tail. With tail threaded on tapestry needle, seam BO and CO edges of second garter stitch section.

Second Ribbed Section

Pick up and knit 48 (56, 64) sts as for First Ribbed Section. Work k1, p1 rib for about 1" (2.5 cm), ending after Needle 3.

Heel

Sl 11 (13, 15) sts from beg of Needle 1 to end of Needle 4; sl rem st from Needle 1 to beg of Needle 2; 25 (29, 33) sts on Needles 2 and 3 will be worked later for instep.

Work short-rows (see Glossary, page 123) on 23 (27, 31) Needle 4 sts only to shape heel as foll:

First Half

Row 1: (RS) K2 (3, 4), make 1 (M1; see Glossary, page 121), [k6 (7, 8), M1] three times, k2, wrap & turn (w & t)—27 (31, 35) sts on Needle 4.

Row 2: Knit to last st on Needle 4, w & t.

Rows 3 and 4: Knit to last st before wrapped st (do not knit across any wrapped sts), w & t.

Rep Rows 3 and 4 nine (eleven, eleven) more times—11 (13, 13) wrapped sts on each side of 5 (5, 9) unwrapped center sts.

Second Half

Row 1: (RS) Knit to first wrapped st, lift wrap from RS onto needle and knit it tog with wrapped st tbl, turn.

Row 2: Sl 1 pwise with yarn in front (wyf), knit to first wrapped st, lift wrap from RS onto needle and knit it tog with wrapped st tbl, turn.

Rep Row 2 twenty (twenty-four, twenty-four) more times; all wraps have been lifted.

Rearrange sts so that 13 (15, 17) sts are on Needle 4 and 14 (16, 18) sts are on Needle 1. Turn to RS and resume working in the rnd—52 (60, 68) sts.

Foot

On Needle 1, work in St st; on Needles 2 and 3, work in k1, p1 rib as established; on Needle 4, work in St st. Work until piece measures 5¾ (6½, 7½)" (14.5 [16.5, 19] cm) from back of heel or about 1¾ (2, 2)" (4.5 [5, 5] cm) less than desired finished length.

Toe

Bottom of Toe

Sl all sts from Needle 4 to Needle 1. Work short-rows over 27 (31, 35) sts on Needle 1 to shape toe.

Rows 1 and 2: Knit to last st on needle, w & t.

Rows 3 and 4: Knit to st before wrapped st (do not knit across any wrapped sts), w & t.

Rep Rows 3 and 4 nine (eleven, eleven) more times—there are now 11 (13, 13) wrapped sts on either side of 5 (5, 9) unwrapped center sts.

Top of Toe

Row 1: (RS) Knit to first wrapped st, lift wrap from RS onto needle and knit it together with the stitch it was wrapped around tbl, turn.

Row 2: Sl1 wyf, knit to first wrapped st, lift wrap from RS onto needle and knit it tog with wrapped st, turn.

Rep Row 2 nineteen (twenty-three, twenty-three) more times (one wrap rem at end of needle).

Next Row: Sl 1 pwise wyf, k1, ssk, knit to last 4 sts, k2tog, k1, lift wrap from RS onto needle and knit it tog with wrapped st tbl—25 (29, 33) sts rem on Needle 1.

Finishing

Sl all sts from Needle 3 to Needle 2—50 (58, 66) sts total; 25 (29, 33) on each Needle 1 and 2. Cut yarn, leaving 18" (45.5 cm) tail.

With tail threaded on tapestry needle, use the Kitchener st (see Glossary, page 120) to graft sts on Needles 1 and 2. Weave in ends. Block lightly.

Split-Toe Sweethearts

Priscilla Gibson-Roberts

Sometimes it can't hurt to just let the yarn take you where it wants to go. Inspired by a gorgeous colorway in reds and pinks, these symmetrical tabi-style socks begin with a charming split toe and end with an intarsia heart motif.

FINISHED SIZE

8½" (21.5 cm) circumference, 9" (23 cm) from back of heel to tip of toe.

NOTE

To change size, measure foot circumference and multiply by 10 sts to find the number of sts required for circumference. Work 40% of circumference sts for big toe and 80% of circumference sts for remaining toes. Work toes ¼" (6 mm) shorter than actual toes, and work foot to ½" (1.3 cm) less than actual foot length measured from tip of longest toe to point of ankle bone.

YARN

Fingering weight (Super Fine #1).
Shown here: Cherry Tree Hill Supersock (100% superwash merino wool; 420 yd [384 m]/4 oz): Foxy Lady (handpaint), 1 skein; black, about 140 yd (119 m), and cherry (red), about 30 yd (28 m).

NEEDLES

U.S. size 0 (2 mm): set of 5 double-pointed (dpn). Adjust needle size if necessary to obtain the correct gauge.

NOTIONS

Stitch holder; tapestry needle.

GAUGE

18 stitches and 26 rounds = 2" (5 cm) in stockinette stitch worked in the round.

✿ Circular Cast-on

This method for casting on for circle in the round is invisible. With the yarn tail held in your left hand, make a loop over your fingers and hold the working yarn between your thumb and index finger (Figure 1). *Insert the needle through the middle of the loop, wrap the working yarn around it, and draw it back through. Yarn over (Figure 2). Rep from * for desired number of sts (Figure 3). This method produces an odd number of sts (Figure 4). Arrange sts on needles and pull tail to snug the circle.

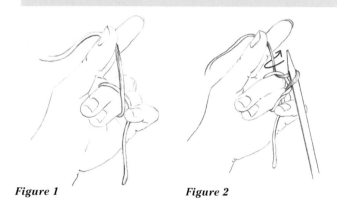

Figure 1   **Figure 2**

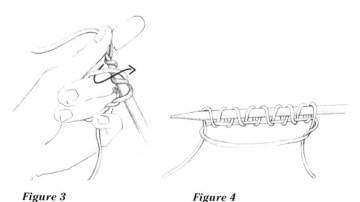

Figure 3   **Figure 4**

Right Sock

Big Toe

With red and using circular method (see illustrations at left), CO 9 sts as foll: make a loop with tail of yarn passing over working yarn from right to left. CO 1 st by passing needle under working yarn, then CO 7 more sts alternating from the inside and outside of the loop.

Arrange sts evenly over 4 dpns (2 sts on each needle). Join for working in the rnd, being careful not to twist sts. Place marker (pm) for beg of rnd. Knit 1 rnd.

Next rnd: [K1, yo] 7 times, k1—16 sts.

Knit one rnd, working yos through back loops (tbl).

Next rnd: [K1, yo] 16 times—32 sts.

Working in St st, begin stripe patt as foll: 8 rnds red, 1 rnd black, 3 rnds red, 2 rnds black, 2 rnds red, 3 rnds black, 1 rnd red, 2 rnds black; piece measures about 1¾" [(4.5 cm). Break yarn; place all sts onto waste yarn to be worked later.

Four Toes

With black, CO and work as for Big Toe for 4 rnds—32 sts. Arrange sts over 3 needles as foll: on Needles 1 and 3, 11 sts; on Needle 2, 10 sts.

Next rnd: On Needle 1, k1, make 1 (M1; see Glossary, page 121), knit to end; on Needle 2, knit; on Needle 3, knit to last st, M1, k1—2 sts inc'd.

Next rnd: Knit.

Rep last 2 rnds 10 times—54 sts; 22 sts on each Needle 1 and 3; 10 sts on Needle 2.

Next rnd: (grafting rnd) On Needle 1, k1, M1, knit to end; slip any 10 Big Toe sts from waste yarn onto spare needle and break yarn, leaving about 12" [30.5 cm] of yarn; graft 10 sts from Needle 2 tog with any 10 sts from Big Toe using Kitchener st (see Glossary, page 121). Rejoin yarn at beg of Needle 3, knit to last st, M1, k1—23 sts on each Needle 1 and 3.

Foot

Next rnd: On Needle 1, knit; with empty needle (Needle 2), pick up and knit 3 sts at graft line, then knit next 11 sts from Big Toe; with another empty needle (now Needle 3) knit rem 11 sts from Big Toe, then pick up and knit 1 st on each side of the grafted sts (1 on Four Toes, 1 on Big Toe), plus 1 st between grafted sts with Needle 4 (previously Needle 3) knit—74 sts.

Next rnd: On Needle 1, k1, M1, knit to end; on Needles 2 and 3, knit; on Needle 4, knit to last st, M1, k1—76 sts.

Cont with black, work even in St st until piece measures 2½" (6.5 cm) from tip of Four Toes.

Change to handpaint and continue in St st until piece measures 7¼" (18.5 cm), or 1¾" (4.5 cm) less than desired total length of foot.

Short-Row Heel

Work short-rows (see Glossary, page 123) on one needle over 38 sts only from Needles 1 and 2 to shape heel as foll:

Heel Base

Change to black; do not cut handpaint.

Row 1: (RS) K37, turn, leaving 1 st unworked.

Row 2: (WS) Yo backward (see Glossary, page 121), purl to last st (do not work last st), turn. (The yo will make a paired st with the first st knitted.)

Row 3: Yo as usual (i.e., bring yarn from front to back), knit to paired sts made by yo of previous row (do not work paired sts), turn.

Row 4: Yo backward, purl to paired sts made by the yo of the previous row (do not work paired sts), turn.

Rep Rows 3 and 4 until 14 unpaired sts rem bet paired sts (16 sts between yo's), ending having worked to the paired sts at the end of a RS (knit) row. Do not turn.

Intarsia Heart Chart

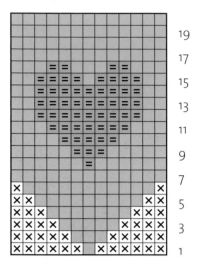

- ☒ With handpaint, knit on RS, purl on WS
- ▢ With black, knit on RS, purl on WS
- ▤ With red, knit on RS, purl on WS

Heel Back

One more st is worked every row so that sts at the sides are gradually worked back in. With the RS still facing, continue with the last row of the heel base as foll:

Row 1: (RS) K1 (the first st of the paired sts), correct the mount of the yo (sl the yo pwise, enter slipped yo with left needle tip from front to back to correct st mount, place on left needle), k2tog (the yo with the first st of the next pair), leaving a yo as the first st on the left needle. Turn.

Row 2: (WS) Yo backward, purl to first set of paired sts, purl the first st of the pair, ssp (the yo with the first st of the next pair; see Glossary, page 120), leaving a yo as the first st on the left needle. Turn.

Row 3: Yo as usual, knit to the first paired st, knit the first st of the pair (the next 2 sts will be yos), correct the mount of the 2 yos, k3tog (the 2 yos with the first st of the next pair), turn.

Row 4: Yo backward, purl to first paired st, purl the first st of the pair (the next 2 sts will be yos), sssp (the 2 yos with the first st of the next pair; see Glossary, page 120), turn.
Rep Rows 3 and 4 until all the yos of the first half have been worked, ending with Row 4. The last turn will bring the RS facing; there will be 1 yo at the end of the heel needle. Cut black, leaving a 12" (30.5 cm) tail.

Leg

Next rnd: (RS) With handpaint (still attached), knit to last st before yo, ssk (the last st with the last yo).
Rejoin for working in the round.
Rearrange sts so there are 19 sts on each of 4 needles, with beg of rnd at the outside edge of the Four Toes. Work in St st for 4½" (11.5 cm). End last rnd after Needle 3.

Intarsia Heart

Rearrange sts over 3 needles and establish Intarsia Heart chart by working back and forth and joining each row as foll:

Row 1: (RS) On Needle 1 (previously Needle 4), k28; on Needle 2 (previously Needle 1), k20; on Needle 3 (previously Needle 2), k2, work 13 sts from Row 1 of Heart Chart, k13, pm in fabric for beg of rnd—28 sts each on Needle 1 and 3; 20 sts on Needle 2; beg of rnd is at back of leg.

Row 2: (WS) Yo, purl to last st in patt (working Intarsia Heart chart as established), p2tog (last st of row with yo from beg of row), turn.

Row 3: Yo, knit to last st in patt (working Intarsia Heart Chart as established), ssk (last st of row with yo from beg of row), turn.
Rep Rows 2 and 3 nine times, then rep Row 2 once more, ending with Row 20 of Intarsia Heart Chart.

Cuff

Once again working in the rnd, work garter st as foll:
With black, knit 1 rnd, purl 1 rnd.
With red, knit 1 rnd, purl 1 rnd.
Repeat the last 4 rnds 2 more times.
With black, knit 1 rnd, purl 1 rnd.
BO all sts knitwise. Cut yarns, leaving a 6" (15 cm) tail for each.

Left Sock

Big Toe, Four Toes, and Foot
Work as for Right Foot.

Short-Row Heel
Work as for Right Sock Heel Base and Heel Back over 38 sts from Needles 3 and 4.

Leg
Next rnd: (RS) With handpaint still attached, knit across heel sts to last st before yo, ssk (the last st with the last yo).

Continue as for Right Sock for 4½" (11.5 cm).

Intarsia Heart
Rearrange sts over 3 needles and establish Intarsia Heart Chart by working back and forth and joining each row as foll:

Row 1: (RS) On Needle 1 (previously Needle 4), k13, work 13 sts in Intarsia Heart Chart, k2; on Needle 2 (previously Needle 1), k20, on Needle 3 (previously Needle 2), k28, pm in fabric for beg of rnd—28 sts each on Needle 1 and 3; 20 sts on Needle 2; beg of rnd is at back of leg.

Continue as for Right Sock, working Intarsia Heart in patt as established.

Cuff
Work as for Right Sock.

Finishing (both socks)
To close the cuff, use black and red tails to make a short twisted cord (see Glossary, page 123) on each sock; tie off with overhand knot. Weave in ends. Block lightly.

Whirlpool Socks

Laura Nelkin

It may be impossible to stop a particular handpainted skein from pooling or striping, so this pattern fools the eye into ignoring it. The swirling textured pattern and bead accents pull attention away from any color patterning. Play around with different bead colors to see which combination creates a cohesive blend between the colors in the yarn.

FINISHED SIZE
About 6½ (7½, 8½)" (16.5 [19, 21.5] cm) foot circumference and 7½ (8¾, 9½)" (19 [22.2, 24 cm]) long from back of heel to tip of toe.

YARN
Fingering weight (Super Fine #1).
Shown here: Schaefer Yarn Anne (60% superwash wool, 25% mohair, 15% nylon; 560 yds [512 m]/4 oz]): Sophia Smith, 1 skein.

NEEDLES
U.S. sizes 0 (2 mm) and 1 (2.25 mm): set of 4 double-pointed (dpn). Adjust needle size if necessary to obtain the correct gauge.

NOTIONS
Marker (m); tapestry needle; 280 (384, 504) size 8° seed beads (about 35 g); bead stringing needle.

GAUGE
18 stitches and 23 rounds = 2" (5 cm) in stockinette stitch worked in the round on larger needles.

NOTE
Before casting on, pre-string the beads. With yarn threaded on a large-eye needle, pick up beads and slide them along the yarn, holding them out of the way of the knitting. When a bead is needed to complete a stitch, slide one down and place it as necessary.

 STITCH GUIDE

Whirlpool Pattern

(mult of 9 sts)

Rnd 1: *Ssk, k5, k1f&b, Bead st (slip next bead along yarn toward needles, k1 wrapping yarn with bead twice around right needle); rep from * to end.

Rnd 2: *Ssk, k5, k1f&b, sl 1 purlwise (pwise) with yarn in back (wyb), dropping wrap; rep from * to end.

Rnd 3: *Ssk, k5, k1f&b, k1; rep from * to end.

Repeat Rnds 1–3 for Whirlpool patt.

Note: When working a bead st, make sure that when you knit the st, the bead is to the front and as close as possible to the right needle.

Whirlpool Chart

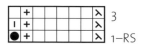

3

1–RS

☐ knit

☒ ssk

⊞ k1f&b

⬤ Bead st (Slip next bead along yarn toward needles, k1 wrapping yarn with bead twice around right needle)

⊡ sl 1 pwise wyb, dropping second wrap

Note: There are only 8 sts shown on this chart but 9 sts are in fact being worked. The k1f&b counts as 2 sts.

Leg

String 140 (192, 252) beads onto yarn for first sock.

With smaller needles, loosely CO 64 (72, 80) sts. Arrange sts as evenly as possible on 3 dpn, place marker (pm), and join for working in the rnd, being careful not to twist sts. Rnd begins at side of leg.

Picot Edge

Knit 9 rnds.

Picot fold line: *K2tog, yo; rep from * to end. Knit 9 rnds. Fold hem in half with WS tog and knit the next st tog with the first st of CO edge. Continue around until all hem sts are joined.

6½" size only

K2tog, knit to end—63 sts rem.

7½" size only

Knit 1 rnd.

8½" size only

Make 1 (M1; see Glossary, page 121), knit to end—81 sts.

All sizes

Change to larger needles and arrange sts as foll: Needle 1: 27 (27, 27) sts; Needle 2: 18 (27, 27) sts; Needle 3: 18 (18, 27) sts.

Work Whirlpool patt 20 (24, 28) times; piece measures about 6 (7, 8)" (15 [18, 20.5] cm) from picot edge and there should be no remaining strung beads.

Heel

Heel Flap

Slip 5 (9, 13) sts from beg of Needle 2 to end of Needle 1; slip 2 (0, 67) sts from beg of Needle 3 to end of Needle 2—32 (36, 40) sts on Needle 1; 15 (18, 21) sts on Needle 2; 16 (18, 20) sts on Needle 3. On Needle 1, k32 (36, 40), turn work so WS is facing, sl 1 pwise with yarn in front (wyf), p31 (35, 39)—32 (36, 40) heel sts are centered at back of leg. Rem 31 (36, 41) sts will be worked later for instep. Work 32 (36, 40) heel sts back and forth in rows as foll:

Row 1: (RS) *Sl 1 knitwise (kwise) with yarn in back (wyb), k1; rep from * to end.

Row 2: Sl 1 pwise wyf, purl to end.

Rep Rows 1 and 2 fifteen (sixteen, seventeen) more times—32 (34, 36) rows worked, 16 (17, 18) chain selvedge sts.

Turn Heel

Work short-rows (see Glossary, page 123) to shape heel as foll:

Row 1: (RS) Sl 1 pwise wyb, k17 (19, 21), ssk, k1, turn.

Row 2: Sl 1 pwise wyf, p5, p2tog, p1, turn.

Row 3: Sl 1 pwise wyb, knit to 1 st before gap produced by previous row, ssk (1 st from each side of gap), k1, turn.

Row 4: Sl 1 pwise wyf, purl to 1 st before gap produced by previous row, p2tog (1 st from each side of gap), p1, turn.

Rep Rows 3 and 4 until all heel sts have been worked ending, with a WS row—18 (20, 22) heel sts rem. On the last 2 rows, omit the k1 or p1 after the dec if necessary.

Shape Gussets

Note: One extra st is picked up along the selvedge in the corner of each heel flap to avoid leaving a hole at the base of the gusset.

Pick up sts along selvedge edges of heel flap and rejoin for working in the rnd as foll:

Rnd 1: With Needle 1, k18 (20, 22) heel sts then pick up and knit 17 (18, 19) sts along selvedge edge of heel flap; with Needle 2, knit across 31 (36, 41) instep sts; with Needle 3, pick up and knit 17 (18, 19) sts along other edge of heel flap, then knit the first 9 (10, 11) heel sts again—83 (92, 101) sts total; 26 (28, 30) sts each on Needles 1 and 3; 31 (36, 41) instep sts on Needle 2. Rnd begins at center back heel.

Rnd 2: On Needle 1, knit to last 3 sts, k2tog, k1; on Needle 2, knit to end; on Needle 3, k1, ssk, knit to end—2 sts dec'd.

Rnd 3: Knit.

Rep Rnds 2 and 3 eleven more times—59 (68, 77) sts rem; 14 (16, 18) sts each on Needles 1 and 3; 31 (36, 41) instep sts on Needle 2.

Foot

Cont even in St st until piece measures about 5¾ (6¾, 7¼)" (15 [17, 19] cm) from back of heel, or about 1¾ (2, 2¼)" [3.8 (5, 5) cm] less than desired total foot length.

6½" size only
M1, knit to end—58 sts.

7½" size only
Knit 1 rnd.

8½" size only
K2tog, knit to end—76 sts rem.

Toe

Redistribute sts on needles as foll:
On Needle 1, 15 (17, 19) sts; on Needle 2, 30 (34, 38) sts; on Needle 3, 15 (17, 19) sts
Work in St st as foll:

Rnd 1: On Needle 1, knit to last 3 sts, k2tog, k1; on Needle 2, k1, ssk, knit to last 3 sts, k2tog, k1; on Needle 3, k1, ssk, knit to end—4 sts dec'd.

Rnd 2: Knit around.

Rep Rnds 1 and 2 five (seven, eight) more times—34 (36, 40) sts rem. Rep Rnd 1 only 6 (6, 7) times—10 (12, 12) sts rem. Knit the sts on Needle 1 onto the end of Needle 3— 5 (6, 6) sts on each 2 needles.

Finishing

Cut yarn, leaving a 12" (30.5 cm) tail. Thread tail on a tapestry needle and use the Kitchener st (see Glossary, page 120) to graft sts tog. Weave in loose ends. Block lightly.

Herringbone Rib Socks

Kristi Schueler

A stitch pattern resembling herringbone weave helps to blend the colors of handpainted yarn; the bold ribs add stretch for a more forgiving fit. This versatile unisex pattern may well become one of the go-to sock patterns in your repertoire.

FINISHED SIZE
About 7½ (9)" (19 [23] cm) foot circumference and 8½ (10)" (21.5 [25.5] cm) long from back of heel to tip of toe.

YARN
Fingering weight (Super Fine #1).
Shown here: Claudia's Hand Painted Yarns Fingering (100% merino; 175 yd [160 m]/50 g): John B., 2 skeins.

NEEDLES
U.S. size 1.5 (2.5 mm): set of 4 double-pointed (dpn). Adjust needle size if necessary to obtain the correct gauge.

NOTIONS
Marker (m); tapestry needle.

GAUGE
14 stitches and 22 rounds = 2" (5 cm) in stockinette stitch worked in the round.

Herringbone Rib Pattern

(mult of 12 sts)

Rnd 1: *P1, k1, [yo, sl 1 purlwise (pwise) with yarn in back (wyb), k2, psso 2 knit sts)] 3 times, p1; rep from * to end.

Rnd 2: *P1, [k2, sl 2 sts just worked back to left-hand needle, pass third st over 2 sts just worked, yo] 3 times, k1, p1; rep from * to end.

Rep Rnds 1 and 2 for patt.

Herringbone Rib Chart

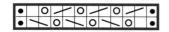

1

☐   knit

⊡   purl

⊙   yo

⊠   slip 1 st pwise wyb, k2 psso the 2 knit sts

⊠   k2, slip them back to left-hand needle pass 3rd st over 2 sts just knitted

☐   pattern repeat

Leg

With larger needles, loosely CO 60 (72) sts. Arrange sts so there are 24 (24) sts on Needle 1, 24 (24) sts on Needle 2, and 12 (24) sts on Needle 3. Place marker (pm) and join for working in the rnd, being careful not to twist sts. Rnd begins at back of leg.

Next rnd: P1, k2, *p2, k2; rep from * to last st, p1. Rep the last rnd 11 more times—12 rnds total; piece measures about 1" (2.5 cm) from CO. Work Herringbone Rib patt until piece measures about 7 (8)" (18 [20.5] cm) from CO, or desired length to top of heel, ending with Rnd 1.

Heel

Sl 1 pwise wyb, k20 (23), turn work so WS is facing, sl 1 pwise with yarn in front (wyf), p29 (35) onto Needle 1, slip any remaining sts to Needle 2 —30 (36) heel sts centered at back of leg. Rem 30 (36) sts will be worked later for instep.

Heel Flap

Work 30 (36) heel sts back and forth in rows as foll:

Row 1: (RS) *Sl 1 pwise wyb, k1; rep from * to end of row.

Row 2: (WS) Sl 1 pwise wyf, purl to end. Rep Rows 1 and 2 thirteen (sixteen) times—30 (36) rows have been worked (including the 2 rows worked above]—15 (18) chain edge sts at each selvedge.

Turn Heel

Work short-rows to shape heel as foll:

Row 1: (RS) Slip 1 pwise wyb, k17 (20), ssk, k1, turn work.

Row 2: Sl 1 pwise wyf, p7, p2tog, p1, turn.

Row 3: Sl 1 pwise wyb, knit to 1 st before gap produced by previous row, ssk (1 st from each side of gap), k1, turn.

Row 4: Sl 1 pwise wyf, purl to 1 st before gap produced by previous row, p2tog (1 st from each side of gap), p1, turn.

Rep Rows 3 and 4 until all heel sts have been worked—18 (22) heel sts rem. On last 2 rows, omit the knit or purl sts after dec if necessary.

Shape Gussets

Pick up and knit sts (see Glossary, page 122) along selvedge edges of heel flap and rejoin for working in the rnd as foll:

Rnd 1: With Needle 1, k18 (22) heel sts then pick up and knit 15 (18) sts along edge of heel flap; with Needle 2, work 30 (36) instep sts as foll: k2 (0), p1 (0), work 24 (36) sts in Herringbone Rib patt as est, p1 (0), k2 (0); with Needle 3, pick up and knit 15 (18) sts along other edge of heel flap, then knit the first 9 (11) heel sts again—78 (94) sts total; 24 (29) sts each on Needles 1 and 3; 30 (36) instep sts on Needle 2. Rnd begins at center of heel.

Rnd 2: On Needle 1, knit to last 3 sts, k2tog, k1; on Needle 2, work in patt as established; on Needle 3, k1, ssk, knit to end—2 sts dec'd.

Rnd 3: Cont in patt as established (work sts on Needle 2 as for Rnd 1; work in St st on Needles 1 and 3).

Rep Rnds 2 and 3 eight (ten) more times—60 (72) sts rem.

Foot

Cont even in patts as established until piece measures about 6¾ (8)" (17 [20] cm) from back of heel, or about 1¾ (2)" (4.5 [5] cm) less than desired total foot length.

Toe

Work in St st as foll:

Rnd 1: On Needle 1, knit to last 3 sts, k2tog, k1; on Needle 2, k1, ssk, knit to last 3 sts, k2tog, k1; on Needle 3, k1, ssk, knit to end—4 sts dec'd.

Rnd 2: Knit.

Rep Rnds 1 and 2 six (eight) more times—32 (36) sts rem. Rep Rnd 1 every rnd 4 (5) times—16 sts rem. Knit the sts on Needle 1 onto Needle 3— 8 sts each on 2 needles.

Finishing

Cut yarn, leaving a 12" (30.5 cm) tail. Thread tail on a tapestry needle and use the Kitchener st (see Glossary, page 120) to graft sts tog. Weave in loose ends. Block lightly.

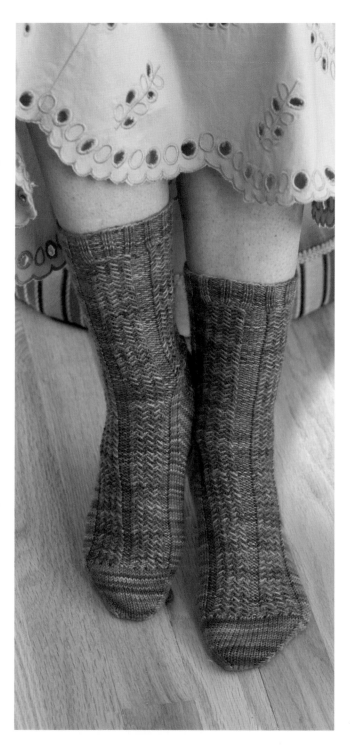

Schooner Socks

Charlene Schurch

One way to combat pooling is to change the length of yarn needed to complete a round. Charlene Schurch reached into her bag of tricks and came up with bobbles, eyelets, and a curving vertical pattern. There's plenty of visual interest in these socks—and they're a fun knit, too!

FINISHED SIZE
About 6 (7½, 9)" foot circumference and 6 (9¾, 10)" (15 [19, 25.5] cm) long from back of heel to tip of toe.

YARN
Fingering weight (Super Fine #1).
Shown here: Colinette JitterBug (100% merino wool; 318 yd [291 m]/110 g): #23 slate, 1, (2, 2) skeins.

NEEDLES
Upper leg—U.S. size 3 (3.0 mm): set of 4 double-pointed (dpn). Lower leg and foot—U.S. size 2 (2.5 mm): set of 4 dpn. Adjust needle size if necessary to obtain the correct gauge.

NOTIONS
Marker (m); tapestry needle.

GAUGE
16 stitches and 22 rounds = 2" (5 cm) in stockinette stitch worked in the rnd on smaller needles.

Make Knot (MK)

(K1, p1, k1, p1, k1) in same st (5 sts on right-hand needle), then pass 2nd, 3rd, 4th, and 5th sts one by one over 1st st (1 st on right-hand needle).

Schooner Pattern

(mult of 12 sts)

Rnd 1: Knit.

Rnd 2 and all even-numbered rnds: Knit.

Rnds 3, 5, 7, 9, and 11: *K2, ssk, k2tog, k1, MK, k2, yo, k1 through back loop (tbl), yo, k1, rep from * to end.

Rnd 13: Knit.

Rnds 15, 17, 19, 21, and 23: K3, yo, k1 tbl, yo, k2, MK, k1, ssk, k2tog.

Rnd 24: Knit.

Rep Rnds 1–24 for Schooner Pattern.

Schooner Chart

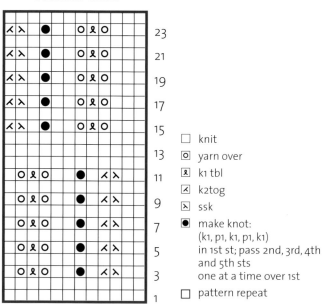

knit

yarn over

k1 tbl

k2tog

ssk

make knot:
(k1, p1, k1, p1, k1)
in 1st st; pass 2nd, 3rd, 4th
and 5th sts
one at a time over 1st

pattern repeat

Leg

With larger needles, loosely CO 48 (60, 72) sts. Divide sts on 3 dpn as follows: 12 (24, 24) sts each on Needles 1 and 3; 24 (12, 24) sts on Needle 2; place marker (pm), and join for working in the rnd, being careful not to twist sts. Rnd begins at back of leg.

Work in k2, p2 rib until cuff measures about 1½" (3.8 cm) from CO. Work Schooner patt until piece measures 4" (10 cm) from CO. Change to smaller needles and cont in Schooner patt until piece measures about 6 (7, 8)" (15 [18, 20.5] cm) from CO, or desired length to start of heel, ending with Rnd 1 or 13 of patt.

Heel

On Needle 1, k12 (18, 18), turn work so WS is facing, sl 1, p23 (29, 35)—24 (30, 36) heel sts centered at back of leg. Rem 24 (30, 36) sts will be worked later for instep; divide them evenly over Needles 2 and 3.

Heel Flap

Work 24 (30, 36) heel sts back and forth in rows on Needle 1 as foll:

Row 1: (RS) *Sl 1 purlwise (pwise) with yarn in back (wyb), k1; rep from * to end.

Row 2: (WS) Sl 1 pwise with yarn in front (wyf), purl to end.

Rep Rows 1 and 2 eleven (fourteen, seventeen) times—12 (15, 18) chain sts at each selvedge edge.

Turn Heel

Work short-rows (see Glossary, page 123) to shape heel as foll:

Row 1: (RS) Sl 1 purlwise (pwise) with yarn in back (wyb), k12 (15, 18), ssk, k1, turn work.

Row 2: Sl 1 pwise with yarn in front (wyf), p3, p2tog, p1, turn.

Row 3: Sl 1 pwise wyb, knit to 1 st before gap produced by previous row, ssk (1 st from each side of gap), k1, turn.

Row 4: Sl 1 pwise wyf, purl to 1 st before gap produced by previous row, p2tog (1 st from each side of gap), p1, turn.

Rep Rows 3 and 4 until all heel sts have been worked—14 (16, 20) heel sts rem. On the last 2 rows, omit the k1 or p1 after the dec if necessary.

Shape Gussets

Pick up and knit sts (see Glossary, page 122) along selvedge edges of heel flap and rejoin for working in the rnd as foll:

Rnd 1: With Needle 1, k14 (16, 20) heel sts, then pick up and knit 12 (15, 18) sts along edge of heel flap; with Needle 2, knit across 24 (30, 36) instep sts; with Needle 3, pick up and knit 12 (15, 18) sts along other edge of heel flap, then knit the first 7 (8, 10) heel sts again—62 (76, 92) sts total; 19 (23, 28) sts each on Needles 1 and 3; 24 (30, 36) instep sts on Needle 2. Rnd begins at center of heel.

Rnd 2: On Needle 1, knit to last 3 sts, k2tog, k1; on Needle 2, knit; on Needle 3, k1, ssk, knit to end—2 sts dec'd.

Rnd 3: Knit.

Rep Rnds 2 and 3 six (seven, nine) times more times—48 (60, 72) sts rem; 12 (15, 18) sts on each Needles 1 and 3; 24 (30, 36) instep sts on Needle 2.

Foot

Cont even in st st as established until piece measures about 4¾ (8¼, 8)" (12 [21, 20.5] cm) from back of heel, or about 1¼ (1½, 2)" (3.2 [3.8, 5] cm) less than desired total foot length.

Toe

Work in St st as foll:

Rnd 1: On Needle 1, knit to last 3 sts, k2tog, k1; on Needle 2, k1, ssk, knit to last 3 sts, k2tog, k1; on Needle 3, k1, ssk, knit to end—4 sts dec'd.

Rnd 2: On Needle 1, knit; on Needle 2, knit; on Needle 3, knit.

Rep Rnds 1 and 2 five (six, eight) more times—24 (32, 36) sts rem. Rep Rnd 1 every rnd 3 (4, 4) times—12 (16, 20) sts rem. Knit the sts on Needle 1 onto the end of Needle 3—6 (8, 10) sts on each of 2 needles.

Finishing

Cut yarn, leaving a 12" (30.5 cm) tail. Thread tail on a tapestry needle and use the Kitchener st (see Glossary, page 120) to graft sts tog. Weave in loose ends. Block lightly.

Corrugated Stripe Socks

Courtney Kelley

Inspired by the traditional two-color corrugated ribbing used in many Fair Isle garments, these socks use one nearly solid and one variegated shade to produce this masterpiece in stripes. The sock is ingeniously constructed so that even heel and toe continue the unbroken line of stripes, while the frequent shifts from solid to multi make pooling a thing of the past.

Finished size
About 7 (8, 9)" (18 [20.5, 23] cm) foot circumference and 9 (9¾, 10½)" (23 [25, 26.5] cm) long from back of heel to tip of toe.

Yarn
Fingering weight (Super Fine #1)
Shown here: Koigu Premium Merino (100% merino wool; 175 yd (160 m)/50 g): [#1125] (plum), 2 skeins. Koigu Painter's Palette Premium Merino (100% merino wool; 175 yd (160 m)/50 g): [#P100L] (multi), 2 skeins.

Needles
Cuff —U.S. size 1 (2.25 mm): set of 5 double-pointed (dpn). Leg, heel, and foot—U.S. size 2 (2.75 mm): set of 5 double-pointed (dpn). I-cord—U.S. size 4 (3.5 mm): set of 2 dpns. Adjust needle size if necessary to obtain the correct gauge.

Notions
Marker (m); stitch holders; tapestry needle.

Gauge
18 sts and 19 rnds = 2" (5 cm) in patt st (after blocking).

Note
Because of the stranded pattern, these socks are less elastic than other patterns. Wash and block your gauge swatch for an accurate measurement. To make the socks smaller or larger, you may wish to increase or decrease the stitch count in multiples of 8 sts. Alternately, using a needle a size smaller or larger may make the socks fit better, but understand that changing the gauge will also change the finished fabric.

STITCH GUIDE

Cuff and Toe Pattern
(mult of 2 sts)
Rnd 1: *With plum, k1; with multi, p1; rep from * to end.
Rep Rnd 1 for Cuff and Toe patt.

Leg Pattern
(mult of 4 sts)
Rnd 1: *With plum, k2, with multi, k2; rep from * to end.
Rep Rnd 1 for Leg patt.

Leg

I-cord edging
With multi and largest needles, provisionally CO 4 sts (see Glossary, page 119). Work in I-cord (see Glossary, page 121) as foll:
Row 1: With plum, knit.
Row 2: With multi, knit.
Rep Rnds 1 and 2 until 64 (72, 80) rows have been worked. Cut yarn, leaving an 8" (20.5 cm) tail. Remove waste yarn from CO and place sts on a dpn. With tail threaded on tapestry needle, use the Kitchener st (see Glossary, page 120) to graft CO and BO of I-cord tog.

Ribbed cuff
With smallest needles, pick up and knit (see Glossary, page 122) 1 st in every row along edge of I-cord, alternating colors to match patt (i.e., pick up and knit with multi in multi row of I-cord; pick up and knit with plum in plum row of I-cord). Arrange sts evenly over 4 dpns so that the first st on every needle is in plum—64 (72, 80) sts; 16 (18, 20) sts on each needle. Place marker (pm) for beg of rnd and join for working in the rnd, being careful not to twist sts. Rnd begins at side of leg.

Work in Cuff and Toe patt (see Stitch Guide) until piece measures 2" (5 cm) from outside edge of I-cord.

Leg
Change to medium-size needles and work Leg patt (see Stitch Guide) until sock measures 7½ (8, 8½)" (19 [20.5, 21.5] cm) from outer edge of I-cord or desired length to top of heel.

Heel
Heel is worked back and forth in rows with 32 (36, 40) sts; rem 32 (36, 40) sts will be worked later for instep.

Heel flap
Setup row: Working in patt as established, k32 (36, 40); move these sts to a holder. On Needle 1, *with plum, k1; with multi, k1; rep from * to end of rnd.
Row 1: (WS) Continuing in heel patt as established, sl 1 purlwise (pwise) with yarn in front (wyf), with plum, p1, *with multi, p1; with plum, p1; rep from * to end.
Row 2: Sl 1 pwise with yarn in back (wyb), with multi, k1, *with plum, k1, with multi, k1; rep from * to end.]
Rep Rows 1 and 2 fifteen (fifteen, twenty-three) times—16 (16, 24) chain edge sts along each selvedge edge.

Turn Heel
Continuing in heel patt as established, work short-rows (see Glossary, page 123) to shape heel as foll:
Row 1: (WS) Sl 1 pwise wyf, p23 (25, 27), turn.
Row 2: Sl 1 pwise wyb, k15, turn.
Row 3: Sl 1 pwise wyf, purl to last st before gap created on previous row; with plum, p2tog (1 st from each side of gap), turn.
Row 4: Sl 1 pwise wyb, knit to last st before gap created on previous row; with multi, ssk (1 st from each side of gap), turn.
Rep Rows 3 and 4 until all sts have been worked, ending with WS (Row 3)—16 (16, 16) heel sts rem on Needle 1.

Shape gussets
Setup Rnd: With Needle 1 and working in Leg patt, k16 heel sts, pick up and knit 16 (16, 24) sts along selvedge edge of heel flap in Leg patt, pm after 8 (8, 12) sts have been picked up; with Needle 2, work 32 (36, 40) instep sts in

Leg patt as established; with Needle 3, pick up and knit 16 (16, 24) sts along second selvedge edge of heel flap working in Leg patt, pm after 8 (8, 12) sts have been picked up, work 8 heel sts from Needle 1. Rnd begins at center of heel—80 (84, 104) sts; 24 (24, 32) sts each on Needles 1 and 3; 32 (36, 40) instep sts on Needle 2.

Rnd 1: On Needle 1, work in pattern to marker, sl m, k2tog using color of second st on left needle, work to end; on Needle 2, work in Leg patt as established; on Needle 3, work in pattern to 2 sts before marker, ssk using color of first st on left needle before ssk, sl m and work in pattern to end of rnd—2 sts dec'd.

Rnd 2: Knit.

Rep Rnds 1 and 2 seven (five, eleven) more times—64 (72, 80) sts total; 16 (18, 20) sts each on Needles 1 and 3; 32 (36, 40) sts on Needle 2.

Foot

Work in Leg patt as established until piece measures 7¼ (7¾, 8¼)" (18.5 [19.5, 21] cm) from back of heel or 1¾ (2, 2¼)" (4.5 [5, 5.5] cm) less than desired finished length.

Begin Toe Shaping

Rnd 1: On Needle 1, work in Cuff and Toe patt to last 3 sts, with multi, k2tog, k1; on Needle 2, with plum, k1, ssk, cont in Cuff and Toe patt to last 3 sts, with multi, k2tog, k1; on Needle 3, with plum, k1, ssk, continue in Cuff and Toe patt to end—4 sts dec'd.

Rnd 2: Knit colors as they appear.

Rep Rnds 1 and 2 six (eleven, thirteen) more times—36 (24, 24) sts rem. Rep Rnd 1 only 5 (2, 2) more times—16 sts rem. Work sts from Needle 1 with Needle 3—8 sts on each of 2 dpns.

Finishing

Cut yarn, leaving a 12" (30.5 cm) tail. With plum tail threaded on tapestry needle, use the Kitchener st to graft sts tog. Weave in ends. Block lightly.

Flame Thrower Socks

Lorna Miser

You can find design inspiration in many unlikely places—even at a motorcycle shop. These socks are inspired by the flickering flames of a popular motorcycle logo. By interspersing the multicolored shade with the solid in changing numbers of stitches, this pattern skillfully disguises any pooling tendencies while creating an eye-catching and unique design.

FINISHED SIZE
About 7½ (8½, 9½)" (19 [21.5, 24] cm) foot circumference and 9½ (11, 13)" (24 [28, 33] cm) long from back of heel to tip of toe.

YARN
Fingering weight (Super Fine #1).
Shown here: Lorna's Laces Shepherd Sock (80% superwash wool, 20% nylon; 215 yd [195 m]/50 g): #16ns charcoal (black), 2 skeins, #146 flames (handpaint), 1 skein.

NEEDLES
U.S. size 1 (2.25 mm): set of 4 double-pointed (dpn). Adjust needle size if necessary to obtain the correct gauge.

NOTIONS
Marker (m); tapestry needle.

GAUGE
15 sts and 21 rnds = 2" (5 cm) in St st worked in the rnd.

NOTE
If desired, work Flame Chart in opposite direction on second sock for symmetry.

Flame Chart

Row numbers (right side of chart, odd numbers): 1, 3, 5, 7, 9, 11, 13, 15, 17, 19, 21, 23, 25, 27, 29, 31, 33, 35, 37, 39, 41, 43, 45, 47, 49, 51, 53, 55, 57

☐ with black, knit
▲ with handpaint, knit
☐ pattern repeat for smallest size
☐ pattern repeat for medium size
☐ pattern repeat for largest size

Leg

With handpaint, loosely CO 56 (64, 72) sts. Divide sts as evenly as possible over 3 dpn, place marker (pm), and join for working in the rnd, being careful not to twist sts. Rnd begins at side of leg. Work in k1, p1 rib for 1" (2.5 cm).

Work Flame Chart in appropriate size for 58 rnds, keeping floats loose across back of work and catching any floats longer than 6 sts long. Cut handpaint yarn. With black only, work for 1" (2.5 cm) or until leg measures desired length to heel.

Heel

Heel is worked back and forth in rows on 28 (32, 36) sts; rem 28 (32, 36) sts will be worked later for instep.

Row 1: (RS) *Sl 1 purlwise (pwise) with yarn in back (wyb), k1, rep from * to end.

Row 2: Sl 1 pwise with yarn in front (wyf), purl to end.

Rep Rows 1 and 2 thirteen (fifteen, seventeen) more times—14 (16, 18) chain sts along each selvedge edge.

Turn Heel

Work in short-rows (see Glossary, page 123) to shape heel as foll:

Row 1: (RS) Sl 1 pwise wyb, k15 (17, 19) sts, ssk, k1, turn.

Row 2: (WS) Sl 1 pwise wyf, p5, p2tog, p1, turn.

Row 3: Sl 1 pwise wyb, knit to last st before gap formed on previous row, ssk (1 st from each side of gap), k1, turn.

Row 4: Sl 1 pwise wyf, purl to last st before gap formed on prev row, p2tog (1 st from each side of gap), p1, turn.

Rep Rows 3 and 4 until all heel sts have been worked—16 (18, 20) heel sts rem.

Shape Gussets

Setup rnd: On Needle 1, k16 (18, 20) heel sts, then pick up and knit (see Glossary, page 122) 14 (16, 18) sts along edge of heel flap, pick up and knit 1 st in corner of heel flap; with Needle 2, knit; with Needle 3, pick up and knit 1 st in corner of heel flap, pick up and knit 14 (16, 18) sts along edge of heel flap, then k8 (9, 10) heel sts from Needle 1—74 (84, 94) sts; 23 (26, 29) sts each on Needles 1 and 3; 28 (32, 36) instep sts on Needle 2. Rnd begins at center of heel.

Rnd 1: On Needle 1, knit to last 3 sts, k2tog, k1; on Needle 2, knit; on Needle 3, k1, ssk, knit to end—2 sts dec'd.

Rnd 2: Knit.

Rep Rnds 1 and 2 eight (nine, ten) more times—56 (64, 72) sts rem.

Foot

Cont even in St st until piece measures about 7¾ (9, 10¾)" (19.5 [23, 27.5] cm) from back of heel, or about 1¾ (2, 2¼)" (4.5 [5, 5.5] cm) less than desired total foot length.

Toe

Work in St st as foll:

Rnd 1: On Needle 1, knit to last 3 sts, k2tog, k1; on Needle 2, k1, ssk, knit to last 3 sts, k2tog, k1; on Needle 3, k1, ssk, knit to end—4 sts dec'd.

Rnd 2: Knit.

Rep Rnds 1 and 2 eight (ten, eleven) more times—20 (20, 24) sts rem.

Work 5 (5, 6) sts from Needle 1 onto Needle 3—10 (10, 12) sts on each of 2 needles.

Finishing

Cut yarn, leaving a 12" (30.5 cm) tail. Thread tail on a tapestry needle and use the Kitchener st (see Glossary, page 120) to graft sts tog. Weave in loose ends. Block lightly.

Chevvy

Jody Pirrello

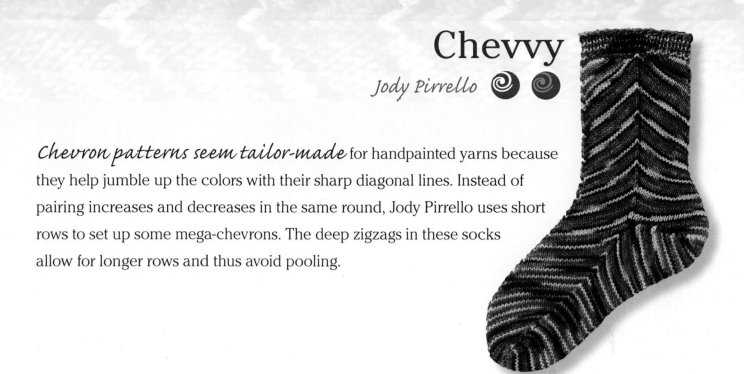

Chevron patterns seem tailor-made for handpainted yarns because they help jumble up the colors with their sharp diagonal lines. Instead of pairing increases and decreases in the same round, Jody Pirrello uses short rows to set up some mega-chevrons. The deep zigzags in these socks allow for longer rows and thus avoid pooling.

FINISHED SIZE
About 7½ (8¼)" (19 [21] cm) foot circumference and 8¼ (10)" (21 [25.5] cm) long from back of heel to tip of toe.

YARN
Fingering weight (Super Fine #1).
Shown here: Fiesta Baby Boom (100% superwash merino wool; 220 yd [209 m]/2 oz): #12148 mochachino, 2 skeins.

NEEDLES
U.S. size 3 (3.25 mm): two 24" (60 cm) circular (cir). Adjust needle size if necessary to obtain the correct gauge.

NOTIONS
2 ring markers and 1 removable st marker (m); tapestry needle.

GAUGE
14 stitches and 20 rounds = 2" (5 cm) in stockinette stitch worked in the round.

Working with Two Circular Needles

Cast the required number of sts onto one circular (cir) needle. Slide sts to opposite end of needle and slip half of the sts onto another cir needle (Needle 1). Slide rem sts on Needle 2 to the flexible cable portion of that needle. With sts still on rigid end of Needle 1, hold Needle 1 in front of Needle 2 in preparation for joining into a round. Join the ends, being careful not to twist sts.

*Take the opposite end of Needle 1, bring it around to the right, and knit the sts off the right side of Needle 1. (Needle 1 will form a circle as sts from the left side are worked onto the right side.) When all sts from Needle 1 have been worked, slide them to the flexible cable portion of the needle. Turn the knitting around and pick up Needle 2. Slide the sts from the flexible cable to the right

tip of Needle 2. Pick up the left side of the needle, bring it around and knit the sts from one side of Needle 2 to the other. (Needle 2 will form a circle as the sts are worked from one side to the other.) Slide the sts to the flexible cable portion of Needle 2 and turn the work, returning to Needle 1. Rep from *.

Leg

Using one cir needle and long-tail method (see Glossary, page 119), loosely CO 64 (72) sts. Place 32 (36) sts onto a second cir needle, and join for working in the rnd with two cir needles (see explanation above), being careful not to twist sts. Rnd begins at side of leg. Work k1, p1 rib for 9 rnds—piece measures about 1" (2.5 cm) from CO.
Setup rnd: * K8 (10), ssk, k5 (7), k2tog, k13, ssk; rep from * once more—6 sts dec'd, 29 (33) sts per needle.

Chevron Setup

Note: The Chevron Setup is worked back and forth in short-rows (see Glossary, page 123) on one cir needle at a time. Work all wraps tog with wrapped sts as you come to them.
Row 1: (RS) K13 (15), k1f&b, place marker (pm), k1f&b, k5, wrap next st, turn (w & t).
Row 2: (WS) P13, w & t.
Row 3: K5, k1f&b, slip marker (sl m), k1f&b, k7, w & t.
Row 4: P17, w & t.
Row 5: K7, k1f&b, sl m, k1f&b, k9, w & t.
Row 6: P21, w & t.
Row 7: K9, k1f&b, sl m, k1f&b, k12, w & t.
Row 8: P27, w & t.
Row 9: K12, k1f&b, sl m, k1f&b, k14, w & t.
Row 10: P31, w & t.

Larger size only:
Row 11: K14, k1f&b, sl m, k1f&b, k17, w & t.
Row 12: P37, w & t.

Both sizes:
Next row: K14 (17), k1f&b, sl m, k1f&b, knit to end—41 (45) sts on Needle 1.
Repeat Chevron Setup on Needle 2—82 (90) sts.
    Use Needle 2 to knit to m on Needle 1 (21 (23) sts), remove m—beg of rnd is now beg of Needle 1. Place removable st marker into knitted fabric to mark beginning of rnd. Rnd begins at back of leg. With Needle 1, k19 (21), sl 2 sts tog as if to knit (sl 2), k1, pass 2 sl sts over knit st (p2sso), k19 (21); with Needle 2, k19 (21), sl 2, k1, p2sso, k18 (20), k1f&b—39 (43) sts on Needle 1 and 40 (44) sts on Needle 2.

Chevron

Note: Chevron is worked in the round.
Rnd 1: With Needle 1, k1f&b, k17 (19), sl 2, k1, p2sso, k17 (19), k1f&b; with Needle 2, k1f&b, k17 (19), sl 2, k1, p2sso, knit to end—39 (43) sts each on Needles 1 and 2.
Rnd 2: With Needle 1, knit to end; with Needle 2, knit to last st, k1f&b—1 st inc'd.

Rep Rnds 1–2 until leg measures 7½" (19 cm) or 1" (2.5 cm) less than desired length from long tip of chevron to base of foot.

Next rnd: Rep Rnd 1.

Next rnd: On Needle 1, knit to end; on Needle 2: k19 (21).

Heel

Heel Flap

Redistribute sts to work heel: Sl 19 (21) sts last worked from Needle 2 to st holder—20 (22) sts rem on Needle 2. Pm, sl first 20 (22) sts from Needle 1 to Needle 2—40 (44) sts on Needle 2. Place held sts on Needle 1. Heel is worked back and forth in rows on Needle 2 only.

Row 1: (RS) Knit to m, sl m, sl 1 purlwise (pwise) with yarn in back (wyb), k12 (14), w & t.

Row 2: (WS) P26 (30), w & t.

Row 3: Knit to m, sl m, sl 1 pwise wyb, k10 (12), w & t.

Row 4: P22 (26), w & t.

Rep Rows 3 and 4 three (four) more times, working 2 fewer sts after m on each RS row and 4 fewer sts on each WS row.

Turn Heel

Work all wraps tog with wrapped sts as you come to them.

Row 1: K5, remove m, k6, w & t.

Row 2: P12, w & t.

Row 3: K13, w & t.

Row 4: P14, w & t.

Row 5: K15, w & t.

Row 6: P16, w & t.

Cont in this manner, repeating Rows 5 and 6, working one more st on each row until the wraps are around the first and last st on the needle, ending with a WS row. With Needle 2, k30 (33), sl rem 9 (10) sts to Needle 1.

Shape Gussets

Gussets are worked in the rnd on Needles 1 and 2.

Setup rnd: On Needle 1 (instep), k7 (8), sl 2, k1, p2sso (picking up wrap and working tog with wrapped st), k17 (19), k1f&b, pm, k1f&b, k17 (19), sl 9 (10) sts from Needle 2 to Needle 1, sl 2, k1, psso, k7 (8); on Needle 2 (sole), knit.

Rnd 1 and all odd–numbered rnds: Knit.

Rnd 2: On Needle 1, k6 (7), sl 2, k1, p2sso, k17 (19), k1f&b, sl m, k1f&b, k17 (19), sl 2, k1, p2sso, knit to end; on Needle 2, knit—2 sts dec'd.

Rnd 4: On Needle 1, k6 (7), sl 2, k1, p2sso, k17 (19), k1f&b, sl m, k1f&b, k17 (19), sl 2, k1, p2sso, knit to end; on Needle 2, knit—2 sts dec'd.

Cont in this manner for 10 (12) more rnds, working 1 fewer st before first dec on each even rnd—40 (44) sts on Needle 1 and 22 (24) sts on Needle 2.

Foot

Rnd 1: Knit.

Rnd 2: With Needle 1, ssk, knit to last st before m, k1f&b, sl m, k1f&b, knit to last 2 sts, k2tog; with Needle 2, knit.

Rep Rnds 1 and 2 until tip of toe is 6¼ (7¼)" or 2 (2½)" (5 [6.5] cm) shorter than desired finished length from back of heel.

Toe

Setup

Rnd 3: Knit.

Rnd 4: With Needle 1, ssk, knit to m, sl m, sl 1 pwise wyb, knit to last 2 sts, k2tog; with Needle 2, knit—2 sts dec'd on Needle 1.

Rep Rnds 1–4 (Rnds 1 and 2 from Foot, Rnds 3 and 4 from Toe Setup) two more times—34 (38) sts rem on Needle 1; 22 (24) sts rem on Needle 2.

Rnd 5: With Needle 1, ssk, k to last 2 sts, k2tog; with Needle 2, knit—2 sts dec'd on Needle 1.

Rnd 6: With Needle 1, ssk, knit to last st before m, k1f&b, sl m, k1f&b, knit to last 2 sts, k2tog, with Needle 2, knit.

Rep Rnds 5–6 two (three) more times—28 (30) sts rem on Needle 1.

Next rnd: With Needle 1, ssk, knit to last 2 sts, k2tog; with Needle 2, knit—26 (28) sts rem on Needle 1.

Next rnd: With Needle 1, ssk, knit to m, sl m, sl 1 pwise wyb, k to last 2 sts, k2tog; with Needle 2, knit—24 (26) sts rem on Needle 1.

Next rnd: With Needle 1, ssk, knit to last 2 sts, k2tog—22 (24) sts rem on each needle.

Bottom of toe

Note: Toe is worked back and forth on Needle 2 only, decreasing sts from Needle 1.

Sl 2 sts from each end of Needle 1 to Needle 2—26 (28) sts on Needle 2; 18 (20) sts on Needle 1.

Row 1: (RS) Knit to last 5 sts, k2tog, k1, ssk, turn—24 (26) sts on Needle 2.

Row 2: (WS) Sl 1 pwise wyf, purl to last 5 sts, ssp, p1, p2tog, turn—22 (24) sts on Needle 2.

Note: The decreases at the end of Rows 3 and 4 are worked with 1 st from Needle 2 and 1 st from Needle 1.

Row 3: Sl 1 pwise wyb, knit to last 4 sts, k2tog, k1, ssk, turn—2 sts dec'd (1 from each needle).

Row 4: Sl 1 pwise wyf, purl to last 4 sts, ssp, p1, p2tog, turn—2 sts dec'd (1 from each needle).

Rep Rows 3 and 4 four (five) times—12 sts rem on Needle 1 and 8 sts rem on Needle 2.

Sl 1 st from each end of Needle 1 onto Needle 2—10 sts rem on each needle.

Finishing

Cut yarn, leaving a 12" (30.5 cm) tail. Thread tail on a tapestry needle and use the Kitchener st (see Glossary, page 120) to graft sts tog. Weave in loose ends. Block lightly.

Spot Check Sock

Beth Parrott

Knit in the simplest of Fair Isle patterns, this sock alternates stitches of two contrasting yarns—every stitch of the bright yarn, as if a precious stone, in a setting of the solid color.

FINISHED SIZE
About 6½ (7½, 9)" (16.5 [19, 23] cm) foot circumference and 8¾ (9½, 10¼)" (22 [24, 26] cm) long from back of heel to tip of toe.

YARN
Fingering weight (Super Fine #1).
Shown here: Shibui Sock (100% superwash merino, 191 yd [175 m]/50 g): #323 peacock (teal; A), 2 skeins, and #51301 spectrum (multi; B), 1 (1, 2) skeins.

NEEDLES
Cuff, heel and toe—U.S. size 2 (2.75 mm): set of 4 double-pointed (dpn). Leg and foot—U.S. size 1 (2.25 mm): set of 4 dpn. Adjust needle size if necessary to obtain correct gauge.

NOTIONS
Tapestry needle.

GAUGE
17 stitches and 22 rounds = 2" (5 cm) in stockinette stitch worked in the round on smaller needles.
18 stitches and 18 rounds = 2" (5 cm) in stockinette stitch worked in patt st in the round on larger needles.

Spot Pattern

(mult of 2 sts + 1)

Rnd 1: *K1 A, k1 B, rep from *, end k1 A.

Rnd 2: *K1 B, k1 A, rep from *, end k1 B.

Rep Rnds 1 and 2 for patt.

Leg

With smaller needles and A, loosely CO 50 (60, 70) sts. Divide sts as evenly as possible on 3 dpn and join for working in the rnd, being careful not to twist sts. Place marker for beginning of round. Work k1, p1 ribbing until work measures 1½ (1¾, 2)" (3.8 [2.5, 5] cm) from CO. On last rnd of ribbing, inc 7 (9, 11) sts evenly spaced—57 (69, 81) sts.

Rearrange sts so that there are 28 (34, 40) sts on Needle 1, 14 (16, 20) on Needle 2, and 15 (17, 21) on Needle 3. Change to larger needles and work Spot patt until piece measures about 6¼ (6¾, 7¼)" (16 [17, 18.5] cm) from CO, ending after Rnd 1. Drop B, but do not cut.

Heel

Turn work so WS is facing—28 (34, 40) heel sts on Needle 1; rem 29 (35, 41) sts will be worked later for instep.

Heel Flap

Change to smaller needles and work back and forth on heel sts in rows with A only as foll:

Row 1: (WS) K3, p25 (31, 37).

Row 2: P3, *sl 1 purlwise (pwise) with yarn in back (wyb), k1; rep from * to last 3 sts, k3.

Rep Rows 1 and 2 thirteen (sixteen, nineteen) more times until a total of 28 (34, 40) rows have been worked—14 (17, 20) garter ridges at each selvedge.

Turn Heel

Work short-rows (see Glossary, page 123) to shape heel as foll:

Row 1: (WS) Sl 1 pwise with yarn in front (wyf), p15 (18, 21), p2tog, p1, turn work.

Row 2: (RS) Sl 1 pwise wyb, k5, ssk, k1, turn.

Row 3: Sl 1 pwise wyf, purl to 1 st before gap produced by previous row, p2tog (1 st from each side of gap), p1, turn.

Row 4: Sl 1 pwise wyb, knit to 1 st before gap produced by previous row, ssk (1 st from each side of gap), k1, turn.

Rep Rows 3 and 4 until all heel sts have been worked—16 (20, 22) heel sts rem. Do not turn after final row. On the last 2 rows, omit k1 or p1 after dec if necessary.

Shape Gussets

With larger needles, pick up sts along selvedge edges of heel flap and rejoin for working in the rnd as foll:

Rnd 1: With A and Needle 1, pick up and knit (see Glossary, page 122) 13 (16, 19) along edge of heel flap sts (1 st between each pair of garter ridges) and 2 sts in corner of heel flap and instep; with both yarns (B should be waiting at this spot) and Needle 2, work in patt as established across 29 (35, 41) instep sts; drop B (carry and weave B behind work or cut, leaving a 6" [15 cm] tail, and reattach where called for below) and on Needle 3 with A only pick up and knit 2 sts in the corner of heel flap and instep, and 13 (16, 19) sts along other edge of heel flap, then knit the first 8 (10, 11) heel sts again—75 (91, 105) sts total; 23 (28, 32) sts each on Needles 1 and 3; 29 (35, 41) instep sts on Needle 2. Rnd begins at center of heel.

Resume working Spot patt with both A and B, *except* that the second to last st on Needle 1 and second st on Needle 3 are always knit in A (this may mean two or even three A sts adjacent to each other) as foll:

Rnd 2: On Needle 1, work 8 (10, 11) sts with A, work in Spot patt to last 3 sts (12 [15, 18] sts), k1 with A (keep this st in A throughout), ssk; on Needle 2, work in patt as established; on Needle 3, k2tog, k1 with A (keep this st in A throughout), beg with B (A, B) work in Spot patt to end (20 [25, 29] sts), ending with A (A, B)—2 sts dec'd

Rnd 3: On Needle 1 and beg with B (B, A), work in Spot patt to last 3 sts, k2tog with A, k1; on Needle 2, work in Spot patt as established; on Needle 3, k1, ssk with A, work Spot patt as established to end—2 sts dec'd.

Rnd 4: On Needle 1, work in Spot patt as established to last 2 sts, k1 with A, k1; on Needle 2, work in Spot patt as established; on Needle 3, k1, k1 with A, work in Spot patt as established.

Rep Rnds 3 and 4 seven (nine, ten) more times—57 (69, 81) sts rem; 14 (17, 20) sts on Needles 1 and 3; 29 (35, 41) sts on Needle 2.

Foot

Cont even in patt, working last st of Needle 1 and first st of Needle 3 in A as established until piece measures about 6½ (6¾, 7)" (16.5 [17, 18] cm) from back of heel, or about 1½ (1¾, 2)" (3.8 [4.5, 5] cm) less than desired total foot length. Cut B, leaving a 6" (15 cm) tail.

Toe

With A only and smaller needles, work in St st as foll:

Setup Rnd: On Needle 1, knit; on Needle 2, knit 14 (17, 20) sts, k2tog, knit to end; on Needle 3, knit—1 st dec'd; 28 (34, 40) sts on Needle 2.

Rnd 1: On Needle 1, knit to last 3 sts, k2tog, k1; on Needle 2, k1, ssk, knit to last 3 sts, k2tog, k1; on Needle 3, k1, ssk, knit to end—4 sts dec'd.

Rnd 2: Knit.

Rep Rnds 1 and 2 six (seven, six) times—28 (36, 52) sts rem. Rep Rnd 1 every rnd 3 (5, 9) times—16 sts rem. Knit the sts on Needle 1 onto the end of Needle 3—8 sts each on 2 needles.

Finishing

Cut yarn, leaving a 12" (30.5 cm) tail. Thread tail on a tapestry needle and use the Kitchener st (see Glossary, page 120) to graft sts tog. Weave in ends. Block lightly.

Potpourri Sock

Deb Barnhill

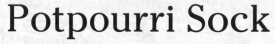

Featuring changing stitch counts, yarnovers, and wrapped stitches, these socks employ all sorts of tricks to combat pooling. Every seventh row features a ribbon of color, created with double figure-eight wrapped stitches. This engaging pattern makes time fly—before you know it, you'll have lovely socks with columns of gently curving arches.

FINISHED SIZE
7½" (8) (19 [20.5] cm) foot circumference; 5½" (14 cm) from cuff turning rnd to top of heel flap; 8½" (21.5 cm) from back of heel to tip of toe.

YARN
Fingering weight (Super Fine #1)
Shown here: Pagewood Farms Chugiak (100% superwash merino wool; 450 yd [411 m]/4 oz): Rainbow, 1 skein.

NEEDLES
U.S. size 1 (2.25 mm): two 20" (51 cm) circular (cir) and set of 4 double-pointed (optional). Adjust needle size if necessary to obtain the correct gauge.

NOTIONS
2 markers (m); tapestry needle.

GAUGE
16 stitches and 23 rounds = 2" (5 cm) in stockinette stitch worked in the round.

Double Figure Eight (DF8)
Note: All slipped sts are worked as if to purl (pwise). [Sl 1 with yarn in back (wyb), move yarn to front between needles, sl 1 with yarn in front (wyf), move yarn to back between needles, sl last st from right needle to left needle wyb, move yarn to front between needles, sl next st from right needle to left needle wyf, move yarn to back] twice, sl 1, k1.

Potpourri Pattern
(mult of 34 sts after end of Rnds 1, 2, 6, or 7; st count varies on other rnds)
Rnd 1: *DF8; rep from * to end.
Rnd 2: Knit.
Rnd 3: *K6, ssk, k1, k2tog, k6; rep from * to end.
Rnd 4: *K6, sl 2 sts tog knitwise (kwise) with yarn in back (wyb), k1, pass 2 sl sts over (p2sso), k6; rep from * to end.
Rnd 5: *K1, yo, k11, yo, k1; rep from * to end.
Rnd 6: *K1, yo, k13, yo, k1; rep from * to end.
Rnd 7: Knit.
Rep Rnds 1–7 for patt.

Cuff
Using the long-tail method (see Glossary, page 119), CO 68 sts loosely over 2 cir held tog. Remove 1 cir, leaving large loops in CO sts. Arrange sts evenly on 2 circular needles, place marker (pm), and join for working in the rnd, being careful not to twist sts. Rnd begins at back of leg.
Rnds 1–4: Knit.
Rnd 5: (turning rnd) *P2tog, yo; rep from * to end.
Rnds 6–10: Knit.
Rnd 11: *K1 tog with loop from CO edge; rep from * to end.

Potpourri Chart
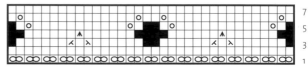

⊂⊃ DF8 (see Stitch Guide)
☐ knit
■ no stitch
⊠ ssk
⊠ k2tog
▲ slip 2 sts tog kwise wyb, k1, p2sso
○ yo
☐ pattern repeat

Leg
Work Rnds 1–7 of Potpourri patt 8 times, then work Rnd 1 once more. Piece measures about 5½" (14 cm) from cuff turning rnd.

Heel
Heel Flap
Next row: K17, turn work, sl 1 pwise wyf, p33—34 sts centered at back of leg for heel flap.
Rearrange sts so that instep sts are on Needle 1 and heel stitches are on Needle 2. Sts on Needle 1 will be worked later for instep. Work 34 heel sts back and forth in rows on Needle 2 as foll:
Row 1: (RS) *Sl 1 pwise wyb, k1; rep from * to end.
Row 2: (WS) Sl 1 pwise wyf, purl to end.
Row 3: Sl 1 pwise wyb, k2, sl 1 pwise wyb, *k1, sl1 pwise wyb; rep from * to last 2 sts, k2.
Row 4: Rep Row 2.
Rep Rows 1–4 six (eight) more times, or to desired heel flap length, ending with Row 4—15 (19) chain sts along each selvedge edge.

Turn Heel
Work short-rows (see Glossary, page 123) to shape heel as foll:
Row 1: (RS) Sl 1 pwise wyb, k18, ssk, k1, turn work.
Row 2: (WS) Sl 1 pwise wyf, p5, p2tog, p1, turn work.

Row 3: Sl 1 pwise wyb, knit 1 st before gap formed on prev row, ssk (1 st from each side of gap), k1, turn work.

Row 4: Sl 1 pwise wyf, purl to 1 st before gap formed on prev row, p2tog (1 st from each side of gap), p1, turn work.

Rep Rows 3 and 4 until all sts have been worked—20 sts rem on Needle 2 with RS facing for next row.

Shape Gussets

Pick up sts along selvedge edges of heel flap and rejoin for working in the rnd as foll:

Rnd 1: With Needle 2 (needle holding heel sts), k20, pick up and knit 1 st in each selvedge st along flap [15 (19) sts], pick up and knit 1 st bet leg and instep; with Needle 1 (needle holding instep sts), k34 (counts as Rnd 2 of Potpourri Chart). With Needle 2, pick up and knit 1 st between instep and leg, pick up and knit 1 st in each selvedge st along edge of heel flap [15 (19) sts], knit to end of needle—86 (94) sts total; 34 instep sts on Needle 1; 52 (60) sole and gusset sts on Needle 2.

Rnd 2: On Needle 1, work in patt as established; on Needle 2, ssk, knit to last 2 sts, k2tog—2 sts dec'd.

Rnd 3: On Needle 1, work in patt as established; on Needle 2, knit.

Rep Rnds 2 and 3 ten (twelve) times more—64 (68) sts rem; 30 (34) sts rem on Needle 2; 30 (34) sts rem on Needle 1 ending with Rnd 3 (7) of Potpourri Chart.

Foot

Continue in patt as established (work Potpourri Chart on Needle 1 and St st on Needle 2) until piece measures 7"

(18 cm) from back of heel or about 1½" (3.8 cm) less than desired foot length, ending with Rnd 3 (Rnd 4) of Potpourri patt—60 sts rem, 30 (26) on Needle 1 and 30 (34) on Needle 2.

Toe

Knit first 5 (3) sts from Needle 1 onto Needle 2, pm, k20, sl last 5 (3) sts pwise from end of Needle 1 to Needle 2; on Needle 2, k20, pm, knit to end—20 sts on Needle 1; 40 sts on Needle 2. Sts are now marked off in 3 sections of 20 sts each.

Note: If desired, transfer each group of 20 sts each to 1 dpn.

With cir

Rnd 1: On Needle 1, ssk, k to last 2 sts, k2tog; on Needle 2, ssk, knit to 2 sts before m, k2tog, sl m, ssk, knit to last 2 sts, k2tog—6 sts dec'd.

Rnd 2: Knit.

With dpns

Rnd 1: On Needle 1, ssk, k to last 2 sts, k2tog; on Needle 2, ssk, knit to last 2 sts, k2tog; on Needle 3, ssk, knit to last 2 sts, k2tog—6 sts dec'd.

Rnd 2: Knit.

Both methods

Rep Rnds 1 and 2 seven times (12 sts rem), then rep Rnd 1 once more—6 sts rem.

Finishing

Cut yarn, leaving a 6" (15 cm) tail, draw through rem sts, and fasten off inside. Weave in ends. Block lightly.

Spread Spectrum

Kristi Schueler

Handpainted yarns look so different when the stitch counts are changed. This is highlighted here by turning the knitting on its side and knitting various widths of intarsia stripes on the leg and contrasting that with standard afterthought heels and wedge toes.

FINISHED SIZE
About 8¾ (9, 9½)" (22 [23, 24] cm) foot circumference and 8 (8¾, 9¼)" (20.5 [22, 23.5] cm) long from back of heel to tip of toe. To fit women's U.S. shoe sizes 6–7½ (women's U.S. shoe sizes 8–9½, women's U.S. shoe sizes 10–11).

YARN
Fingering weight (Super Fine #1)
Shown here: Blue Moon Fiber Arts Socks That Rock Lightweight (100% merino; 360 yd [329 m]/128 g): Blarney Stone, 1 (2, 2) skeins.

NEEDLES
U.S. size 1 (2.25 mm): straight or circular plus set of 5 double-pointed (dpn). Adjust needle size if necessary to obtain the correct gauge.

NOTIONS
Waste yarn; B/1 (2.25 mm) crochet hook; 2 markers (m); tapestry needle.

GAUGE
16 stitches and 23 rows = 2" (5 cm) in stockinette stitch worked in rows.

NOTE
Due to the construction of this sock, the foot and leg circumference should match as closely as possible to the actual foot circumference measurement and the length should be 10% to 15% smaller than the actual foot length measurement. The row gauge is very important for proper foot and leg circumference of this pattern; stitch gauge is important for the length of the foot.

STITCH GUIDE

Edging Pattern
(panel of 7 sts inc'd to 9 sts)

Row 1: (RS) BO 2 sts, 1 st rem on right-hand needle, k3, yo, k2tog, k1—7 sts.

Row 2: (WS) K3, yo, k2tog, [yo] twice, k2—9 sts.

Row 3: K2, (k1, p1) into double yo, k2, yo, k2tog, k1—9 sts.

Row 4: K3, yo, k2tog, k4—9 sts.

Rep Rows 1–4 for Edging patt.

Edging Chart

	knit on RS, purl on WS
■	BO
⊙	yarnover
⊠	k2tog
•	purl on RS, knit on WS
	pattern repeat

Stitch Setup

Foot sts 32 (38, 40) sts	gap for heel	Leg sts 48 sts all sizes						
		F 6 sts	E 4 sts	D 12 sts	C 6 sts	B 4 sts	A 9 sts	A 7 Edging sts

Setup

Wind six yarn butterflies (see Glossary, page 123) of the following lengths: 25, 7, 10, 17, 7, 7 yd (23, 6.5, 9, 15.5, 6.5, 6.5 m). Retain the order of the butterflies, which will be referred to as A–F and used to knit the leg. *Note:* If you are measuring the butterflies using a niddy-noddy or otherwise under tension, add 10% to account for the elasticity of the yarn.

First Half of Sole and Leg Back

With waste yarn, crochet hook, and using the crochet provisional method (see Glossary, page 119) loosely CO 85 (91, 93) sts.

Row 1: (RS) Drop the first 2 crochet chains off left-hand needle. With straight or circular needles, and yarn from A, knit Row 1 of Edging patt, skipping the 2 BO stitches, place marker (pm) for edging, k9; with B, k4; with C, k6; with D, k12; with E, k4; with F, k6, pm for foot, drop two crochet chains; attach ball of yarn and k32 (38, 40) sts for foot, drop rem 2 chains from left needle—80 (86, 88) sts on needle.

Row 2: (WS) Purl, being sure to cross yarns at joins (see Glossary for intarsia, page 122); do not join foot to leg. Continue following Edging patt for the edging as established.

Row 3: Work in patt as established, twisting yarns at the intarsia joins and not joining foot to leg.

Rows 4–12: Rep Rows 2 and 3 four times, then rep Row 2 once more (ending after a WS row).

Short-Rows for Calf Width

Work short-rows (see Glossary, page 123) as foll, continuing Edging patt as established. *Note:* These rows do not contribute to the total row count.

Short-row 1: (RS) Work to edging marker, sl m, k9, wrap & turn (w & t).

Short-row 2: (WS) Sl 1 purlwise (pwise) with yarn in front (wyf), purl.

Short-row 3: Work to edging marker, sl m, k8, w & t.

Short-row 4: Sl 1 pwise wyf, purl.

Short-row 5: Work to edging marker, sl m, k7, w & t.

Short-row 6: Sl 1 pwise wyf, purl.

Resume Leg

Row 13: (RS) Continue Edging patt as established, knit to first wrapped stitch, work wrap tog with st tbl; rep for each wrapped st; work to end of row as established.

Row 14: (WS) Purl to end of row, continuing Edging patt as established.

Row 15: Continue Edging patt, knit to end of row as established.

Rows 16–25 (27, 29): Repeat Rows 14 and 15 five (six, seven) times (ending after a RS row).

Instep and Leg Front

Rows 26 (28, 30): (WS) Purl, continuing with yarn for foot through the first intarsia section of the lower leg (6 sts of Butterfly F), and remove m for foot. Cut F. Continue established patt to end of row.

Row 27 (29, 31): (RS) Work Edging patt and intarsia as established in previous row.

Rows 28 (30, 32)–75 (79, 81): Rep last 2 rows 24 (25, 25) times, ending after a RS row.

Second Half of Heel and Leg Back

Row 76 (80, 82): (WS) Purl 32 (38, 40) sts, pm for foot, reattach F, and continue established intarsia and Edging patt.

Row 77 (81, 83): Work in established pattern, keeping leg and foot stitches separate.

Rows 78 (82, 84)–88 (94, 98): Rep last row 11 (13, 15) times (ending with a WS row).

Repeat Short-rows 1–6.

Row 89 (95, 99): (RS) Rep Row 13.

Row 90 (96, 100): Rep Row 14.

Row 91 (97, 101): Rep Row 15.

Rows 93 (99, 103)–100 (104, 108): Rep Rows 14 and 15 three (two, two) times, then rep Row 14 once more (ending with a WS row).

Join

Remove provisional CO and place freed sts on a spare needle. Hold needles parallel, with fabric folded in half with wrong sides together. Thread the tail from of A (the first intarsia section) on tapestry needle and beg with Edging patt, use the Kitchener st (see Glossary, page 120) to graft the the CO and BO edges tog. Cut yarn from foot sts, leaving a 2 yd (1.8 m) tail. With tail threaded on tapestry needle, graft the CO and BO edges of the foot in the same manner as the leg.

Heel

Pick up and knit sts (see Glossary, page 122) for heel as foll:

Holding sock with RS of edging facing you, beg at bottom right of heel opening, and using dpns, pick up and knit 35 (36, 38) sts along leg edge of heel. Arrange sts as evenly as possible on 2 dpns. Turn sock so edging faces away from you and pick up and knit 35 (36, 38) sts along foot edge of heel. Arrange sts as evenly as possible on 2 dpns—70 (72, 78) heel sts.

Rnd 1: On Needles 1 and 3, k1, ssk, knit to end; on Needles 2 and 4, knit to last 3 sts, k2tog, k1—4 sts dec'd.

Rnd 2: Knit.

Rep Rnds 1 and 2 eight (eight, nine) more times—34 (36, 38) sts rem. Rep Rnd 1 only five times—14 (16, 18) sts rem. Slip sts from Needle 2 to Needle 1 and sts from Needle 4 to Needle 3—7 (8, 9) sts on each needle. Cut yarn, leaving a 12" (30.5 cm) tail. With tail threaded on tapestry needle, and use the Kitchener St to graft rem sts tog.

Toe

With sole facing and beg at the right of toe opening, work as for heel.

Finishing

Weave in loose ends. Block lightly.

Braided Gem Socks

Elizabeth Ravenwood

These socks use a braided rib, which looks like a cable but is knitted without a cable needle, to create vertical interest and distract the eye from the yarn's horizontal striping effect. Extra elasticity in the leg gives great flexibility in fit and makes this pair comfortable as well as attractive.

FINISHED SIZE
About 7½ (9½)" (19 [24] cm) foot circumference and 9¼ (10½)" (23.5 [26.5] cm) long from back of heel to tip of toe.

YARN
Fingering weight (Super Fine #1).
Shown here: Colinette JitterBug (100% merino wool; 320 yd [291 m]/110 g): #55 Toscana, 1 (2) ball(s).

NEEDLES
U.S. size 2 (2.75 mm): set of 4 double-pointed (dpn). Adjust needle size if necessary to obtain the correct gauge.

NOTIONS
Marker (m); tapestry needle.

GAUGE
15 stitches and 21 rounds = 2" (5 cm) in stockinette stitch worked in the rnd.

 STITCH GUIDE

Braid Pattern

(mult of 7 sts)

Rnds 1 and 3: *P3, k4; rep from * to end.

Rnd 2: *P3, [sl 1 purlwise (pwise) with yarn in back (wyb), k1, yo, pass sl st over knit st and yo] twice; rep from * to end.

Rnd 4: *P3, k1, sl 1 pwise wyb, k1, yo, pass sl st over knit st and yo, k1; rep from * to end

Braid Chart

3

1

☐ knit

⊡ purl

⧄ sl 1 pwise wyb, k1, yo, pass sl st over knit st and yo

☐ pattern repeat

Instep Braid Chart

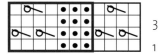

3

1

Leg

Using the cable method (see Glossary, page 118), loosely CO 63 (75) sts. Arrange sts evenly on 3 dpns (21 [25] sts on each needle), place marker (pm), and join for working in the rnd, being careful not to twist sts. Rnd begins at side of leg.

Work in k2, p1 ribbing for 10 (12) rnds. Piece measures about ¾ (1)" (2 [2.5] cm) from CO.

Larger size only

Rnd 13: K1, k1f&b, p1, [k2, p1] eleven times, k1, k1f&b, p1, [k2, p1] twelve times—77 sts.

Both sizes

Work Braid patt until leg measures 6 (8)" (15 [20.5] cm) from CO or desired length to heel, ending with Rnd 4.

Heel

Heel Flap

K31 (38) sts onto 1 dpn (Needle 1). Divide rem 32 (39) sts between 2 dpns; these sts will be worked later for instep. Heel flap is worked back and forth in rows on Needle 1 only. Turn work so WS is facing.

Smaller size only

Row 1: (WS) Sl 1 pwise with yarn in front (wyf), purl to end.

Row 2: (RS) *Sl 1 pwise wyb, k1; rep from * to end.

Rep Rows 1 and 2 thirteen more times—14 chain sts on each selvedge edge of heel flap.

Larger size only

Row 1: (WS) Sl 1 pwise with yarn in front (wyf), purl to end.

Row 2: (RS) *Sl 1 pwise wyb, k1; rep from * to last st, k1.

Rep Rows 1 and 2 seventeen more times—18 chain sts on each selvedge edge of heel flap.

Turn Heel

Work short-rows (see Glossary, page 123) to shape heel as foll:

Row 1: (WS) P17 (21), p2tog, p1, turn work.

Row 2: Sl 1 pwise wyb, k 5 (6), ssk, k1, turn.

Row 3: Sl 1 pwise wyf, purl to 1 st before gap produced on prev row, p2tog (1 st from each side of gap), p1, turn.

Row 4: Sl 1 pwise wyb, knit to 1 st before gap produced on prev row, ssk (1 st from each side of gap), k1, turn.

Rep Rows 3 and 4 until all heel sts have been worked—19 (22) heel sts rem. On the last 2 rows, omit the knit or purl st after dec if necessary.

Shape Gussets

Pick up sts along selvedge edges of heel flap and rejoin for working in the rnd as foll:

Rnd 1: With Needle 1 (needle holding heel sts), pick up and knit (see Glossary, page 122) 1 st at the corner of the heel, 14 (18) sts along heel flap in chain edge sts, and 1 st between heel flap and instep (16 [20] sts); with Needle 2, work 32 (39) instep sts in patt as established; with Needle 3, pick up and knit 1 st between instep and heel flap, 14 (18) sts along other edge of heel flap in chain edge sts, and 1 st in corner of heel, then k9 (11) heel sts from Needle 1— 83 (101) sts total; 26 (31) sts on Needle 1; 32 (39) instep sts on Needle 2; 25 (31) sts on Needle 3. Rnd begins at center of heel.

Rnd 2: On Needle 1, knit to last 2 sts, k2tog; on Needle 2, work in patt as established; on Needle 3, ssk, knit to end—2 sts dec'd.

Rnd 3: On Needle 1, knit; on Needle 2, work in patt as established; on Needle 3, knit.

Rep Rnds 2–3 nine (eleven) more times—63 (77) sts remain.

Foot

Cont in patt as established, working Braid patt on instep sts and stockinette on sole sts, until piece measures about 7 (8)" (18 [20.5] cm) from back of heel, or about 2 (2½)" (5 [6.5] cm) less than desired total foot length.

Toe

Work in St st as foll:

Setup rnd: On Needle 1, knit; on Needle 2, k15 (19), k2tog, k15 (18); on Needle 3, knit—62 (76) sts.

Rnd 1: On Needle 1, knit to last 3 sts, k2tog, k1; on Needle 2, k1, ssk, knit to last 3 sts, k2tog, k1; on Needle 3, k1, ssk, knit to end—4 sts dec'd.

Rnd 2: Knit.

Rep Rnds 1 and 2 ten (twelve) more times—18 (24) sts remain. Knit the sts from Needle 1 onto the end of Needle 3—9 (12) sts on each of two needles.

Finishing

Cut yarn, leaving a 12" (30.5 cm) tail. Thread tail on a tapestry needle and use the Kitchener st (see Glossary, page 120) to graft sts tog. Weave in loose ends. Block lightly.

Escher Socks

Lorna Miser

A ribbed traveling stitch pattern makes these handsome unisex socks stylish. The interlocking rib, reminiscent of Escher patterns, isn't merely good-looking—it also ensures a comfy fit. The simple textured stitch will look good in a wide range of yarns.

FINISHED SIZE
About 7½ (8½)" (19 [21.5] cm) foot circumference and 8½ (10)" (21.5 cm) long from back of heel to tip of toe.

YARN
Fingering weight (Super Fine #1).
Shown here: Lorna's Laces Shepherd Sock (80% wool, 20% nylon; 215 yd [195 m]/50 g): #112 Sand Ridge, 2 skeins.

NEEDLES
U.S. size 1 (2.25 mm): set of 4 double-pointed (dpn). Adjust needle size if necessary to obtain the correct gauge.

NOTIONS
Cable needle (cn; optional); marker (m); tapestry needle.

GAUGE
14 stitches and 17 rounds = 2" (5 cm) in stockinette stitch worked in the round.

Traveling Rib Stitch Pattern
(mult of 4 sts)

Rnds 1–5: *P1, k2, p1; rep from *.
Rnd 6: *Sl 1 st to cn and hold in back of work, k1, purl held st from cn, sl next st to cn and hold in front of work, p1, knit held st from cn; rep from *.
Rnds 7–11: *K1, p2, k1; rep from *.
Round 12: *Sl 1 st to cn and hold in front of work, p1, knit held st from cn, sl 1 st to cn and hold in back of work, k1, purl held st fron cn; rep from *.

Traveling Rib Chart

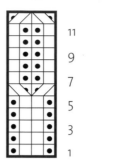

☐ knit
⊡ purl
⬜ hold 1 st in back of work, k1, purl held st
⬜ hold 1 st in front of work, p1, knit held st
☐ pattern repeat

Leg
Loosely CO 52 (60) sts. Divide sts as evenly as possible on 3 dpn, place marker (pm), and join for working in the rnd, being careful not to twist sts. Rnd begins at back of leg. Work Traveling Rib Stitch patt until piece measures about 7 (8)" (18 [20.5] cm) from CO or desired length to heel, ending after Rnd 6 or 12.

Heel
Heel is worked back and forth in rows over 26 (30) stitches. Rem 26 (30) sts will be worked later for instep.

Row 1: (RS) *Sl 1 purlwise (pwise) with yarn in back (wyb), k1; rep from * to end.
Row 2: (WS) Sl 1 pwise with yarn in front (wyf), purl to end.
Rep Rows 1 and 2 twelve (fourteen) more times—13 (15) chain sts along each selvedge edge.

Turn Heel
Work short-rows (see Glossary, page 123) to shape heel as foll:

Row 1: (RS) Sl 1 pwise wyb, k14 (16), ssk, k1, turn work.
Row 2: (WS) Sl 1 pwise wyf, p5, p2tog, p1, turn.
Row 3: Sl 1 pwise wyb, knit to last st before gap formed on prev row, ssk (1 st from each side of gap), k1, turn.
Row 4: Sl 1 pwise wyf, purl to last st before gap formed on prev row, p2tog (1 st from each side of gap), p1, turn.
Rep Rows 3 and 4 until all sts have been worked—16 (18) heel sts rem.

Shape Gussets
Pick up sts along selvedge edges of heel flap and rejoin for working in the rnd as foll:

Rnd 1: With Needle 1, k16 (18) heel sts, then pick up and knit 13 (15) sts along edge of heel flap, then 1 st in the corner of the heel flap; with Needle 2, work 26 (30) instep sts as for Rnd 1 or 7 of Traveling Rib Stitch patt; with Needle 3, pick up and knit 1 st in corner of heel flap, then 13 (15) sts along edge of heel flap, then knit the first 8 (9) heel sts again—70 (80) sts total; 22 (25) sts each on Needles 1 and 3; 26 (30) instep sts on Needle 2. Rnd begins at center of heel.
Rnd 2: On Needle 1, knit to last 3 sts, k2tog, k1; on Needle 2, work in patt as established; on Needle 3, k1, ssk, knit to end—2 sts dec'd.
Rnd 3: With Needle 1, knit; with Needle 2, work in patt as established; with Needle 3, knit.
Rep Rnds 2 and 3 eight (nine) more times—52 (60) sts rem; 13 (15) sts on each Needles 1 and 3; 26 (30) instep sts on Needle 2.

Foot

Cont even in patt as established until piece measures about 6¾ (8)" (17 [20.5] cm) from back of heel or about 1¼ (2)" (4.5 [5] cm) less than desired total foot length, ending after Rnd 6 or 12 of Traveling Rib Stitch patt.

Toe

Work in St st as foll:

Rnd 1: On Needle 1, knit to last 3 sts, k2tog, k1; on Needle 2, k1, ssk, knit to last 3 sts, k2tog, k1; on Needle 3, k1, ssk, knit to end—4 sts dec'd.

Rnd 2: Knit.

Rep Rnds 1 and 2 seven (eight) more times—20 (24) sts rem.

Finishing

Cut yarn, leaving a 12" (30.5 cm) tail. Thread tail on a tapestry needle and use the Kitchener st (see Glossary, page 120) to graft sts tog. Weave in loose ends. Block lightly.

Goldengrove Socks

Mindy Soucek

Vertical interest is created with eyelets and ribs in these sleek socks loosely inspired by the Leafy Trellis pattern from *The Harmony Guides: Lace & Eyelets*. These undulating ribbed socks cushion your feet with subtle yet striking style.

FINISHED SIZE
About 7¼ (8½)" (18.5 [21.5] cm) foot circumference and about 9¼ (10¼)" (23.5 [26] cm) long from back of heel to tip of toe.

YARN
Fingering weight (Super Fine #1).
Shown Here: Dream In Color Smooshy (100% superwash wool; 450 yd [411 m]/4 oz): strange harvest VS130, 1 skein.

NEEDLES
U.S. size 2 (2.75 mm): set of 4 double-pointed (dpn). Adjust needle size if necessary to obtain the correct gauge.

NOTIONS
Marker (m); tapestry needle.

GAUGE
18 stitches and 27 rounds = 2" (5 cm) in stockinette stitch worked in the round. 22 stitches and 24 rounds = 2" (5 cm) in ribbed pattern worked in the round.

Goldengrove Pattern

Rnd 1: *[K1 through back loop (tbl), p1] twice, (k1, p1) 4 times; rep from * to end.

Rnd 2: *K1 tbl, yo, k1, yo k1 tbl, p1, [k1, p1] 4 times; rep from * to end.

Rnd 3: *K1 tbl, sl 1, k2tog, psso, k1 tbl, p1, [k1, p1] 4 times; rep from * to end

Rnds 4–7: Rep Rnds 2 and 3.

Rnd 8: [K1, p1] 3 times, [k1 tbl, p1] twice, *[k1, p1] 4 times, [k1 tbl, p1] twice; rep from * to last 2 sts, k1, p1.

Rnd 9: [K1, p1] 3 times, k1 tbl, yo, k1, yo, k1 tbl, p1, *[k1, p1] 4 times, k1 tbl, yo, k1, yo, k1 tbl, p1; rep from * to last 2 sts, k1, p1.

Rnd 10: [K1, p1] 3 times, k1 tbl, sl 1, k2tog, psso, k1 tbl, p1, *[k1, p1] 4 times, k1 tbl, sl 1, k2tog, psso, k1 tbl, p1; rep from * to last 2 sts, k1, p1.

Rnds 11–14: Rep Rnds 9 and 10.

Goldengrove Chart

13
11
9
7
5
3
1

- ⊠ k1 tbl
- ■ no stitch
- ⊡ purl
- □ knit
- ⊙ yo
- ⋋ sl, k2tog, psso
- □ pattern repeat

Leg

CO 72 (84) st. Arrange sts evenly over 3 needles—24 (28) sts on each needle. Place marker (pm) and join for working in the rnd, being careful not to twist sts. Work k1, p1 rib for 1" (2.5 cm).

Work Rnds 1–14 of Goldengrove patt (see Stitch Guide) 4 (5) times; then work Rnds 1–7 one time—leg measures about 6½ (7½)" (16.5 [19] cm) or desired length to top of heel, ending with Rnd 7 or 14.

Heel

Heel is worked back and forth in rows over 36 (42) sts; rem 36 (42) sts will be worked later for instep. Sl 12 (14) sts from beg of Needle 2 to end of Needle 1.

Heel flap

Row 1: (RS) *Sl 1 purlwise (pwise) with yarn in back (wyb), k1; rep from * to end.

Row 2: Sl 1 pwise with yarn in front (wyf), purl to end.

Rep Rows 1 and 2 eighteen (nineteen, twenty) times—38 (42) rows worked, 19 (21) chain edge sts at each selvedge edge.

Turn heel

Work short-rows (see Glossary, page 123) to shape heel as foll:

Row 1: (RS) Sl 1 pwise wyb, k19 (22), ssk, k1, turn.

Row 2: Sl 1 pwise wyf, p5, p2tog, p1, turn.

Row 3: Sl 1 pwise wyb, knit to gap created on previous row, ssk (1 st from each side of gap), k1, turn.

Row 4: Sl 1 pwise wyf, purl to gap created on previous row, p2tog (1 st from each side of gap), p1, turn

Rep Rows 3 and 4 until all sts have been worked—20 (24) heel sts rem. On the last 2 rows, omit k1 or p1 after dec if necessary.

Shape gussets

Rnd 1: With Needle 1, k20 (24) heel sts, then pick up and knit (see Glossary, page 122) 19 (21) sts along edge of heel flap; with Needle 2, work 36 (42) instep sts in Goldengrove patt as established beg with Rnd 8 or 1; with Needle 3, pick up and knit 19 (21) sts along other edge of heel flap, then k10 (12) sts from Needle 1—94 (108) sts total; 29 (33) sts on each Needle 1 and 3; 36 (42) sts on Needle 2. Pm for beg of rnd and resume working in the rnd.

Rnd 2: On Needle 1, knit to last 3 sts, k2tog, k1; on Needle 2, work in patt as established; on Needle 3, knit—1 st dec'd.

Rnd 3: On Needle 1, knit; on Needle 2, work in patt as established; on Needle 3, k1, ssk, knit to end—1 st dec'd.

Rep Rnds 2 and 3 ten (eleven) more times—72 (84) sts rem; 18 (21) sts each on Needles 1 and 3; 36 (42) sts on Needle 2.

Foot

Cont even in patt as established on instep and work St st on sole until foot measures about 7½ (8)" (19 [20.5] cm) from back of heel or 1¾ (2¼)" (4.5 [5.5] cm) less than desired foot length, ending with Rnd 7 or 14 of patt. Knit 1 rnd.

Toe

Rnd 1: On Needle 1, knit to last 3 sts, k2tog, k1; on Needle 2, k1, ssk, knit to last 3 sts, k2tog, k1; on Needle 3, k1, ssk, knit to end—4 sts dec'd.

Rnd 2: Knit.

Rep Rnds 1 and 2 eight (eleven) more times—36 sts rem, then rep Rnd 1 five more times—16 sts rem.

Finishing

Sl sts from Needle 3 to Needle 1—8 sts each on Needles 1 and 2. Cut yarn, leaving a 12" (30.5 cm) tail. With tail threaded on tapestry needle, use the Kitchener st (see Glossary, page 120) to graft toe sts tog. Weave in ends. Block lightly.

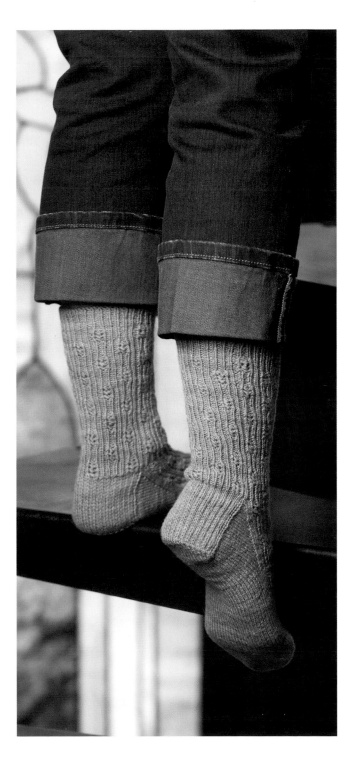

Rib Fantastic

Barb Brown

Columns of zigzagging eyelets are interspersed with columns of stockinette stitch to create these handsome yet comfortable ribbed socks. The undulating pattern swirls the colors around and creates vertical visual interest. You won't be satisfied with making just one pair of these truly fantastic socks!

FINISHED SIZE
About 8 (9)" (20 [22.5] cm) foot circumference and about 8¾" (22 cm) long from back of heel to tip of toe.

YARN
Fingering weight (#1 Super Fine).
Shown here: Koigu Painter's Palette Premium Merino (100% wool, 175 yd [160 m]/50 g): #P530, 2 skeins.

NEEDLES
U.S. size 2 (2.75 mm): set of 4 double-pointed (dpn). Adjust needle size if necessary to obtain the correct gauge.

NOTIONS
Marker (m); tapestry needle.

GAUGE
15 stitches and 18 rounds = 2" (5 cm) in stockinette stitch worked in the round.

STITCH GUIDE

Rib Fantastic Pattern
(mult of 12 [11] sts)

Rnd 1 and all odd-numbered rnds: Knit.

Rnds 2, 4, 6, 8, 10, and 12: *K1, [yo, k2tog] 4 times, k3 (2); rep from * to end.

Rnds 14, 16, 18, 20, 22, and 24: *K1, [ssk, yo] 4 times, k3 (2); rep from * to end.

Rib Fantastic Chart

```
                                    23
                                    21
                                    19
                                    17
                                    15
                                    13
                                    11
                                     9
                                     7
                                     5
                                     3
                                     1
```

☐ knit

⊡ yarnover

☒ k2tog

☒ ssk

▢ pattern repeat for smaller size

▢ pattern repeat for larger size

Leg

Loosely CO 60 (66) sts. Arrange sts so that there are 24 (22) sts on Needle 1, 24 (22) sts on Needle 2, and 12 (22) sts on Needle 3. Place marker (pm) and join for working in the rnd, being careful not to twist sts. Rnd begins at back of leg.

Next rnd: *K2, p2; rep from * to end (*k1, p2, k2, p2, k2, p2: rep from * to end). Rep the last rnd 13 more times—14 rnds total; piece should measure about 1½" (3.75 cm) from CO.

Work Rib Fantastic patt 2 times for a total of 48 rnds, then rep Rnds 1–13 once more; piece measures about 6½" (16.5 cm) from CO.

Heel

Heel Flap

8" size only

Knit first 8 sts from Needle 1 onto Needle 3. Sl last 10 sts of Needle 2 to beg of Needle 3—30 sts on Needle 3. Heel flap is worked over 30 sts on Needle 3; rem 30 sts on Needles 1 and 2 will be worked later for instep. Turn work and purl across heel sts.

9" size only

Knit first 10 sts from Needle 1 onto Needle 3—32 sts now on Needle 3. Turn work and purl across heel sts and at the same time inc 2 sts evenly spaced—34 sts. Heel flap is worked over 34 sts on Needle 3; rem 34 sts on Needles 1 and 2 will be worked later for instep.

All Sizes

Work 30 (34) heel sts back and forth in rows as foll:

Row 1: (RS) *Sl 1 knitwise (kwise) with yarn in back (wyb), k1; rep from * to end.

Row 2: (WS) Sl 1 purlwise (pwise) with yarn in front (wyf), purl to end.

Rep Rows 1 and 2 until 26 (32) rows have been worked—13 (16) chain edge sts at each selvedge.

Turn Heel

Work short-rows to shape heel as foll:

Row 1: (RS) K15 (18), ssk (see Glossary, page 120), k1, turn work—1 st dec'd.

Row 2: (WS) Sl 1 pwise wyf, p1 (3), p2tog, p1, turn—1 st dec'd.

Row 3: Sl 1 pwise wyb, knit to 1 st before gap produced by previous row, ssk (1 st from each side of gap), k1, turn—1 st dec'd.

Row 4: Sl 1 pwise wyf, purl to 1 st before gap produced by previous row, p2tog (1 st from each side of gap), p1, turn—1 st dec'd.

Rep Rows 3 and 4 until all heel sts have been worked—16 (18) heel sts rem. *Note:* On the larger size, omit the last k1 and p1.

Shape Gussets

Pick up sts along selvedge edges of heel flap and rejoin for working in the rnd as foll:

Rnd 1: With Needle 1, k16 (18) heel sts, then pick up and knit (see Glossary, page 122) 14 (17) sts along edge of heel flap; with Needle 2, work across 30 (34) instep sts as follows: K4 (1), work Rib Fantastic patt 2 (3) times, k2 (0); with Needle 3, pick up and knit 14 (17) sts along other edge of heel flap, then knit the first 8 (9) heel sts again—74 (86) sts total; 22 (26) sts each on Needles 1 and 3; 30 (34) instep sts on Needle 2. Rnd begins at center of heel.

Rnd 2: With Needle 1, knit to last 3 sts, k2tog, k1; with Needle 2, work in patt as established; with Needle 3, k1, ssk, knit to end—2 sts dec'd.

Rnd 3: With Needle 1, knit; with Needle 2, work in patt as established; with Needle 3, knit.

Rep Rnds 2 and 3 six (eight) more times—60 (68) sts rem, 30 (34) sts on Needle 2, 15 (17) sts each on Needles 1 and 3.

Foot

Cont even in established patt on instep sts and St st on sole sts until piece measures 7¾ (7½)" (19.5 [19] cm) from back of heel or about 1¾ (2)" (4.5 [5] cm) less than desired total foot length, ending with a knit round.

Toe

Work in St st as foll:

Rnd 1: On Needle 1, *Sl 1 kwise wyb, k1; rep from * to last 3 sts, k2tog, k1; on Needle 2, k1, ssk, sl 1 kwise wyb, k1; rep from * to last 3 sts, k2tog, k1; on Needle 3, k1, ssk, sl 1 kwise wyb, k1; rep from * to end—4 sts dec'd.

Rnd 2: Knit.

Rep Rnds 1 and 2 seven (eight) more times, then rep Rnd 1 once—24 (28) sts rem.

Next rnd: On Needle 1, knit to last 2 sts, k2tog; on Needle 2, p1, ssk, knit to last 3 sts, k2tog, p1; on Needle 3, ssk, knit to end—20 (24) sts remain.

Knit sts from Needle 1 onto the end of Needle 3—10 (12) sts each on 2 needles.

Finishing

Cut yarn, leaving a 12" (30.5 cm) tail. Thread tail on a tapestry needle and use the Kitchener st (see Glossary, page 120) to graft sts tog. Weave in loose ends. Block lightly.

Switcheroo Socks

Carol J. Sulcoski

These socks help diffuse the potential pooling of handpainted yarn by breaking up the colors with double rows of eyelets. The scalloped edging and unusual heel stitch pattern add a touch of extra flair. The first swatch used the other side of the eyelet rib pattern as the right side, but the inside was so attractive that it deserved to be on the outside! Thus the Switcheroo Socks were born.

FINISHED SIZE

About 5¾ (6½, 7½, 8½)" (14.5 [16.5, 19, 21.5] cm) foot circumference and about 7 (8½, 9½, 10½)" (18 [21.5, 25.5, 26.5] cm) foot length from back of heel to tip of toe (unstretched).

YARN

Fingering weight (Super Fine #1).
Shown here: Black Bunny Fibers Superwash Merino Sock (100% superwash wool; 400 yd [366 m]/100 g): Nana's Lilacs, 1 skein.

NEEDLES

U.S. size 3 (3.25 mm): set of 4 double-pointed (dpn). Adjust needle size if necessary to obtain the correct gauge.

NOTIONS

Marker (m); tapestry needle.

GAUGE

15 stitches and 24 rounds = 2" (5 cm) in stockinette stitch worked in the round.

STITCH GUIDE

Reverse Eyelet Rib Pattern

(mult of 6 sts)

Rnds 1–3: *P1, k3, p1, k1; rep from *.
Rnd 4: *P1, yo, k3tog, yo, p1, k1; rep from *.
Repeat Rnds 1–4 for pattern.

Reverse Eyelet Rib Chart

	knit
⊡	purl
⊙	yo
⊿	k3tog
	pattern repeat

Leg

CO 44 (55, 66, 77) sts loosely. Arrange sts over 3 needles so that there are 22 (11, 22, 33) sts on Needle 1 and 11 (22, 22, 22) sts each on Needle 2 and 3. Place marker (pm) and join for working in the rnd, being careful not to twist sts. Rnd begins at side of leg.

Scalloped edging

Rnds 1 and 2: Knit.
Rnd 3: *(P2tog) twice, make 1 right (M1R; see Glossary, page 120), k1, make 1 left (M1L; see Glossary, page 120), k1, M1R, k1, M1L, p2tog twice; rep from * to end of rnd.
Rnds 4–5: Knit.
Rnd 6: Purl.
Rnd 7: Knit.
Rnd 8: Knit, dec 0 (1, 2, 3) st(s) evenly—44 (54, 64, 74) sts rem.

Cuff

Work k1, p1 rib for 8 (9, 10, 11) rnds.
Next rnd: Knit, dec 2 (6, 10, 8) sts evenly—42 (48, 54, 66 sts) rem.
Arrange sts so that there are 18 (24, 18, 18) sts on Needle 1 and 12 (12, 18, 24) sts on Needles 2 and 3.
 Work Reverse Eyelet Rib patt until leg measures 6½ (6¾, 7, 7¼)" (16.5 [17, 18, 18.5] cm) or desired length from CO, ending with Rnd 3 of patt.

Heel

Heel Flap

Sl 2 (0, 4, 6) sts from end of Needle 3 to Needle 1; sl 2 (0, 4, 6) sts from beg of Needle 2 to Needle 1. Heel flap is worked over on 22 (24, 26, 30) sts on Needle 1 only; rem 10 (12, 14, 18) sts each on Needles 2 and 3 will be worked later for instep. Work heel sts back and forth in rows as foll:
Row 1: (RS) Sl 1 pwise wyb, k1, *sl 1 st pwise with yarn in front (wyf), k1; rep from * to end.
Row 2: Sl 1 pwise wyf, purl to end.
Row 3: Sl 1 pwise wyb, *sl 1 pwise wyf, k1; rep from * to last st, k1.
Row 4: Rep Row 2.
Rep these Rows 1–4 six (seven, eight, nine) more times, ending with Row 4—14 (16, 18, 20) chain edge sts.

Turn Heel

Work short-rows (see Glossary, page 123) to shape heel as foll:
Row 1: (RS) Sl 1 purlwise (pwise) with yarn in back (wyb), k12 (13, 14, 16), ssk, k1, turn work.
Row 2: Sl 1 pwise with yarn in front (wyf), p5, p2tog, p1, turn work.
Row 3: Sl 1 pwise wyb, knit to 1 st before gap formed on previous row, ssk (1 st from each side of gap), k1, turn.
Row 4: Sl 1 pwise wyf, purl to 1 st before gap formed on previous row, p2tog (1 st from each side of gap), p1, turn.
Rep Rows 3 and 4 until all heel sts have been worked, ending with a WS row and omitting last k1 or p1 on last 2 rows if necessary—14 (14, 16, 18) sts rem.

Shape Gussets

Note: If desired, you may pick up one extra st along the selvedge in the corner of each heel flap to avoid leaving a hole at the base of the gusset.

Rejoin for working in the rnd as foll:

Rnd 1: With Needle 1, knit across 14 (14, 16, 18) heel sts, then pick up and knit 14 (16, 18, 20) sts along edge of heel flap; with Needle 2, work across 20 (24, 28, 36) instep sts as foll: k4 (0, 2, 0), work 12 (24, 24, 36) in patt as established, k 4 (0, 2, 0); with Needle 3, pick up and knit 14 (16, 18, 20) sts along other edge of heel flap, then knit across the first 7 (7, 8, 9) heel sts from Needle 1 again—62 (70, 80, 94) sts total; 21 (23, 26, 29) sts each on Needles 1 and 3; 20 (24, 28, 36) instep sts on Needle 2. Rnd begins at center of heel.

Rnd 2: On Needle 1, knit to last 3 sts, k2tog, k1; on Needle 2, work all instep sts in patt as established; on Needle 3, k1, ssk, knit to end—2 sts dec'd.

Rnd 3: On Needle 1, knit; on Needle 2, work in patt as established; on Needle 3, knit.

Rep Rnds 2 and 3 eight (ten, eleven, fourteen) times—44 (48, 56, 64) sts remain; 12 (12, 14, 14) sts each on Needles 1 and 3; 20 (24, 28, 36) sts on Needle 2.

Foot

Cont even in patt as established until piece measures 5¾ (7, 7¾, 8½)" (14.5 [18, 19.5, 21.5] cm) from back of heel, or about 1¼ (1½, 1¾, 2)" (3.2 [3.8, 4.5, 5] cm) less than desired total foot length, ending with Rnd 3 of Reverse Eyelet Rib patt on instep sts. Work 2 rnds in St st on all needles.

Smallest size only

Sl 1 from end of Needle 1 to Needle 2; sl 1 from beg of Needle 3 to Needle 2—11 sts rem on each Needle 1 and 3; 22 sts on Needle 2.

Largest size only

Sl 2 from beg of Needle 2 to end of Needle 1; sl 2 from end of Needle 3 to beg of Needle 1—16 sts rem on each Needle 1 and 3; 32 sts on Needle 2.

Toe

Rnd 1: On Needle 1, knit to last 3 sts, k2tog, k1; on Needle 2, k1, ssk, work to last 3 sts, k2tog, k1; on Needle 3, k1, ssk, knit to end—4 sts dec'd.

Rnd 2: Knit.

Rep Rnds 1 and 2 five (five, six, ten) more times—20 (24, 28, 20) sts rem. Rep Rnd 1 every rnd 2 (3, 4, 2) more times–12 sts rem. Knit the sts from Needle 1 onto Needle 3—6 sts each on 2 needles for top and bottom of toe.

Finishing

Cut yarn, leaving a 12" (30.5 cm) tail. Thread tail on a tapestry needle and use the Kitchener st (see Glossary, page 120) to graft sts tog. Weave in loose ends. Block lightly.

glossary

ABBREVIATIONS

beg	beginning; begin; begins	rnd(s)	round(s)
BO	bind off	RS	right side
CC	contrasting color	sl	slip
cm	centimeter(s)	sl st	slip st (slip 1 st pwise unless otherwise indicated)
cn	cable needle		
CO	cast on	ssk	slip 2 sts kwise, one at a time, from the left to right needle, insert left needle tip through both front loops and knit together from this position (1 st decrease)
dec(s)	decrease(s); decreasing		
dpn	double-pointed needles		
foll	follow(s); following		
g	gram(s)	ssp	slip 2 sts kwise, one at a time, from left to right needle, sl these sts tog back to left needle pwise, purl these sts tog through their back loops
inc(s)	increase(s); increasing		
k	knit		
k1f&b	knit into the front and back of same st	sssp	slip 3 sts kwise, one at a time, from left to right needle, sl these sts tog back to left needle pwise, purl these sts tog through their back loops
kwise	knitwise, as if to knit		
m	marker(s)		
MC	main color	st(s)	stitch(es)
mm	millimeter(s)	St st	stockinette stitch
M1	make one (increase)	tbl	through back loop
p	purl	tog	together
p1f&b	purl into front and back of same st	WS	wrong side
patt(s)	pattern(s)	wyb	with yarn in back
pm	place marker	wyf	with yarn in front
prev	previous	yd	yard(s)
psso	pass slipped st over	yo	yarn over
pwise	purlwise, as if to purl	*	repeat starting point
rem	remain; remaining	**	repeat all instructions between asterisks
rep	repeat(s)	( )	alternate measurements and/or instructions
rev St st	reverse stockinette stitch	[ ]	instructions are worked as a group a specified number of times.

Bind-offs

Sewn Bind-Off

This method, popularized by Elizabeth Zimmermann, forms an exceedingly elastic edge that has a ropy appearance, much like a purl row. Cut the yarn three times the width of the knitting to be bound off, and thread onto a tapestry needle. Working from right to left, *insert tapestry needle purlwise (from right to left) through the first two stitches (Figure 1) and pull the yarn through, bring the needle knitwise (from left to right) through first stitch (Figure 2), pull the yarn through, and slip this stitch off the knitting needle. Repeat from *.

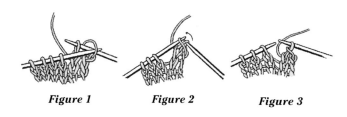

Figure 1　　　　　*Figure 2*

Standard Bind-Off

Knit the first stitch, *knit the next stitch (two stitches on right needle), insert left needle tip into first stitch on right needle (Figure 1) and lift this stitch up and over the second stitch (Figure 2) and off the needle (Figure 3). Repeat from * for the desired number of stitches. If you find that the bound-off edge is too tight, try binding off with a larger needle than the one with which the piece was knitted.

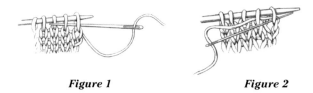

Figure 1　　　*Figure 2*　　　*Figure 3*

Cast-Ons

Backward-Loop Cast-On

*Loop working yarn and place it on needle backward so that it doesn't unwind. Repeat from *.

Cable Cast-On

Hold needle with working yarn in your left hand with the wrong side of the work facing you. *Insert right needle between the first two stitches on left needle (Figure 1), wrap yarn around needle as if to knit, draw yarn through (Figure 2), and place new loop on left needle (Figure 3) to form a new stitch. Repeat from * for the desired number of stitches, always working between the first two stitches on the left needle.

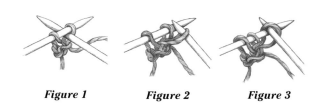

Figure 1　　　*Figure 2*　　　*Figure 3*

Double-Start Cast-On

Make a slipknot and place it on the right needle, leaving a long tail. Place the thumb and index finger of your left hand between the two strands and secure them with your other three fingers. *Release the yarn around the thumb and re-wrap it from above in the opposite direction (Figure 1). With the needle, go straight down and catch the thread behind the thumb, go over the thread around the index finger, and bring the needle back through the thumb loop (Figure 2). Drop the loop off the thumb and, placing your thumb back in the original V position, to tighten up the resulting stitch on the needle. Cast on one stitch as for the Long-Tail method. Repeat from * for the desired number of stitches.

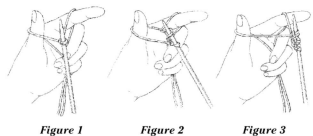

Figure 1　　　*Figure 2*　　　*Figure 3*

Eastern Cast-On

Hold two double-pointed needles parallel to each other. Leaving a 6" (15 cm) tail, wrap the working yarn around both needles counterclockwise (Figure 1) half as many times as the desired number of stitches. (For example, to cast on twelve stitches, wrap the yarn around the needles six times.) To begin knitting, bring the yarn forward between the two needles and use a third needle to knit across the wraps on the top needle (Figure 2). Rotate the two needles so that the needle that had been on the bottom is now on top; use the free needle to knit across the wraps on the top needle (Figure 3).

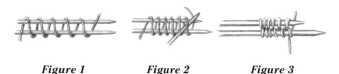

Figure 1   *Figure 2*   *Figure 3*

Long-Tail (Continental) Cast-On

Leaving a long tail (about ½" [1.3 cm] for each stitch to be cast on), make a slipknot and place on right needle. Place thumb and index finger of your left hand between the yarn ends so that working yarn is around your index finger and tail end is around your thumb and secure the yarn ends with your other fingers. Hold your palm upwards, making a V of yarn (Figure 1). *Bring needle up through loop on thumb (Figure 2), catch first strand around index finger, and go back down through loop on thumb (Figure 3). Drop loop off thumb and, placing thumb back in V configuration, tighten resulting stitch on needle (Figure 4). Repeat from * for the desired number of stitches.

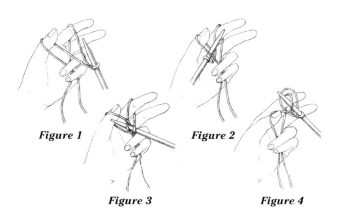

Figure 1   *Figure 2*

Figure 3   *Figure 4*

Provisional (Crochet) Cast-On

With waste yarn and a crochet hook, make a loose crochet chain of about four stitches more than you need to cast on. With knitting needle, working yarn, and beginning two stitches from end of chain, pick up and knit one stitch through the back loop of each crochet chain (Figure 1) for desired number of stitches. Work the piece as desired, and when you're ready to work in the opposite direction, pull out the crochet chain to expose live stitches (Figure 2).

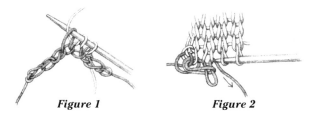

Figure 1   *Figure 2*

Provisional (Invisible) Cast-On

Make a loose slipknot of working yarn and place it on the right needle. Hold a length of waste yarn next to the slipknot and around your left thumb; hold working yarn over your left index finger. *Bring right needle forward under waste yarn, over working yarn, grab a loop of working yarn (Figure 1), then bring needle to the front over both yarns and grab a second loop (Figure 2). Repeat from * for the desired number of stitches. When you're ready to work in the opposite direction, place the exposed loops on a knitting needle as you pull out the waste yarn.

Figure 1   *Figure 2*

Crochet
Crochet chain

Make a slipknot and place it on crochet hook. *Yarn over hook and draw through loop on hook. Repeat from * for the desired number of stitches. To fasten off, cut yarn and draw end through last loop formed.

Decreases

K2tog

Knit two stitches together as if they were a single stitch.

P2tog

Purl two stitches together as if they were a single stitch.

Ssk

Slip two stitches individually knitwise (Figure 1), insert left needle tip into the front of these two slipped stitches, and use the right needle to knit them together through their back loops (Figure 2).

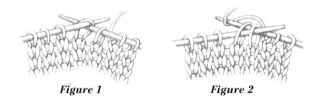

Figure 1   **Figure 2**

Ssp

Holding yarn in front, slip two stitches individually knitwise (Figure 1), then slip these two stitches back onto left needle (they will appear twisted) and purl them together through their back loops (Figure 2).

Figure 1   **Figure 2**

Sssp

Work as for ssp (above), but slip three stitches individually, then purl them together through their back loops.

Embroidery

Lazy daisy

*Bring threaded needle out of knitted fabric from back to front, form a short loop, and insert needle into background where it came out. Keeping the loop under the needle, bring the needle back out of the background a short distance away (Figure 1), pull loop snug, and insert needle into fabric on far side of loop. Repeat from * for desired number of petals (Figure 2; six petals shown).

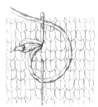

Figure 1

Figure 2

Grafting

Kitchener Stitch

Arrange stitches on two needles so that there is the same number of stitches on each needle. Hold the needles parallel to each other with right sides of the knitting facing up. Allowing about ½" (1.3 cm) per stitch to be grafted, thread matching yarn on a tapestry needle. Work from right to left as follows:

Step 1. Bring tapestry needle through the first stitch on the front needle as if to purl and leave the stitch on the needle (Figure 1).

Step 2. Bring tapestry needle through the first stitch on the back needle as if to knit and leave that stitch on the needle (Figure 2).

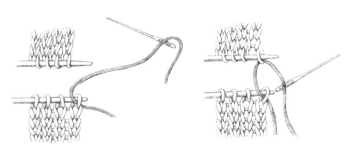

Figure 1   **Figure 2**

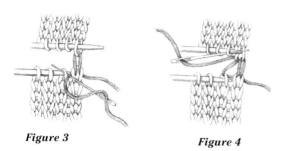

Figure 3   **Figure 4**

Step 3. Bring tapestry needle through the first front stitch as if to knit and slip this stitch off the needle, then bring seaming needle through the next front stitch as if to purl and leave this stitch on the needle (Figure 3).

Step 4. Bring tapestry needle through the first back stitch as if to purl and slip this stitch off the needle, then bring tapestry needle through the next back stitch as if to knit and leave this stitch on the needle (Figure 4).

Repeat Steps 3 and 4 until no stitches remain on the needles, adjusting the tension to match the rest of the knitting as you go.

I-Cord

Using 2 double-pointed needles, cast on the desired number of stitches (usually three to four). *Without turning the needle, slide stitches to other end of needle, pull the yarn around the back, and knit the stitches as usual. Repeat from * for desired length.

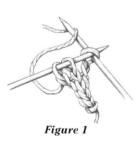

Figure 1

Increases
K1f&b

Knit into a stitch but leave it on the left needle (Figure 1), then knit through the back loop of the same stitch (Figure 2) and slip the original stitch off the needle.

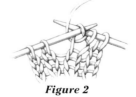

Figure 1   **Figure 2**

Make One Left (M1L)

With left needle tip, lift the strand between last knitted stitch and first stitch on left needle from front to back (Figure 1), then knit the lifted loop through the back (Figure 2). If no slant is specified, use M1L.

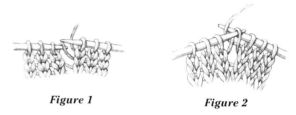

Figure 1   **Figure 2**

Make One Right (M1R)

With left needle tip, lift the strand between last knitted stitch and first stitch on left needle from back to front (Figure 1), then knit the lifted loop through the front (Figure 2).

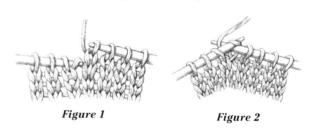

Figure 1   **Figure 2**

Yarnover (yo)

Wrap the working yarn around the needle from front to back, then bring yarn into position to work the next stitch (leave it in back if a knit stitch follows; bring it under the needle to the front if a purl stitch follows).

Yarnover backward (backward yo)

Bring the yarn to the back under the needle, then over the top to the front so that the leading leg of the loop is at the back of the needle. (When worked in a sock heel, the mount of the yarnover will be corrected later; working it backward initially results in a tighter yarnover that gives greater symmetry.)

Intarsia

Intarsia is worked using a separate length of yarn for each section. Cut the yarn into lengths as directed and wind yarn butterflies to keep them tidy. Work across the first section of stitches with the first yarn butterfly and drop it when you come to the next section. Pick up the next yarn butterfly and pass it under the butterfly last used to interweave the sections to prevent a gap at the join, then work across to the next section. Repeat to the end of the row, then turn and work back in the same manner. (Intarsia is almost always worked back and forth in rows.)

Pick Up and Knit

With right side facing and working from right to left, insert tip of needle under the front half (Figure 1) or both halves (Figure 2) of stitch along selvedge edge, wrap yarn around needle, and pull it through to form a stitch on the needle. For a tighter join, pick up the stitches and knit them through the back loop (Figure 3).

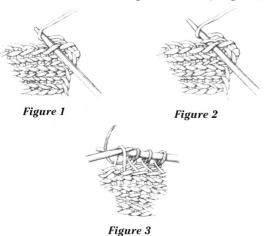

Figure 1   *Figure 2*

Figure 3

Seams
Invisible Horizontal Seam

Working with the bound-off edges opposite each other, right sides of the knitting facing you, and working into the stitches just below the bound-off edges, bring threaded tapestry needle out at the center of the first stitch (i.e., go under half of the first stitch) on one side of the seam, then bring needle in and out under the first whole stitch on the other side (Figure 1). *Bring needle into the center of the same stitch it came out of before, then out in the center of the adjacent stitch (Figure 2). Bring needle in and out under the next whole stitch on the other side (Figure 3). Repeat from *, ending with a half-stitch on the first side.

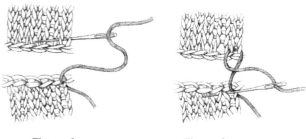

Figure 1   *Figure 2*

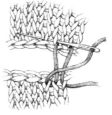

Figure 3

Short-Rows
Short-Rows Knit Side

Work to turning point, slip next stitch purlwise to right needle, then bring the yarn to the front (Figure 1). Slip the same stitch back to the left needle (Figure 2), turn the work around and bring the yarn in position for the next stitch, wrapping the slipped stitch with working yarn as you do so. When you come to a wrapped stitch on a subsequent row, hide the wrap by working it together with the wrapped stitch as follows: Insert right needle tip under the wrap (from the front if wrapped stitch is a knit stitch; from the back if wrapped stitch is a purl stitch), then into the stitch on the needle, and work the stitch and its wrap together as a single stitch.

Figure 1   **Figure 2**

Short-Rows Purl Side

Work to the turning point, slip the next stitch purlwise to the right needle, bring the yarn to the back of the work (Figure 1), return the slipped stitch to the left needle, bring the yarn to the front between the needles (Figure 2), and turn the work so that the knit side is facing—one stitch has been wrapped and the yarn is correctly positioned to knit the next stitch. To hide the wrap on a subsequent purl row, work to the wrapped stitch, use the tip of the right needle to pick up the wrap from the back, place it on the left needle (Figure 3), then purl it together with the wrapped stitch.

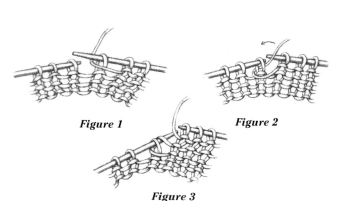

Figure 1   **Figure 2**

Figure 3

Twisted Cord

Trim two lengths of yarn even (Figure 1). Twist each strand individually in the same direction and by the same amount until the yarn begins to kink back on itself. Hold the two strands taut next to each other and release them, allowing them to twist together. Cut two lengths of yarn as specified in pattern. Knot the strands together at each end. Attach one end to a hook or door handle and insert a knitting needle through the other end. Twist the needle (Figure 1); the tighter the twist, the firmer the finished cord will be. Holding the cord in the center with one hand (you may need some help), bring both ends of cord together, allowing the two halves to twist together (Figure 2). Keep the cord straight and avoid tangling. Knot the cut ends together and trim.

Figure 1

Figure 2

Yarn Butterfly

Leaving a 4" (10 cm) tail of yarn across your palm, wrap the other end of the yarn around your thumb and little finger in a figure eight until all the yarn has been wound. Remove the figure eight and wrap the tail around the center of the butterfly a few times (Figure 1), then secure with a slipknot (Figure 2). Knit from the other end of the butterfly.

Figure 1   **Figure 2**

sources

Arucania
Distributed in the United
   States by Knitting Fever
   International
PO Box 336
315 Bayview Ave.
Amityville, NY 11701
(516) 546-3600
knittingfever.com
   Ranco Multi
   Ranco Solid

Black Bunny Fibers
blackbunnyfibers.com
   Superwash Merino Sock

Blue Moon Fiber Arts
56587 Mollenhour Rd.
Scappoose, OR 97056
(503) 922-3431
(866) 802-9687
bluemoonfiberarts.com
   Seduction
   Socks That Rock
   Lightweight

Cherry Tree Hill Yarn
100 Cherry Tree Hill Ln.
Barton, VT 05822
(802) 525-3311
cherryyarn.com
   Supersock
   Supersock Solids

Classic Elite Yarns
122 Western Ave.
Lowell, MA 01851
(978) 453-2837
classiceliteyarns.com
   Alpaca Sox

**Claudia Hand Painted
Yarns**
40 West Washington St.
Harrisonburg, VA 22802
(540) 433-1140
claudiaco.com
   Fingering

Colinette Yarns
Distributed in the United
   States by Unique Kolours
28 North Bacton Hill Rd.
Malvern, PA 19355
(610) 644-4885
(800) 25-2DYE4
uniquecolours.com
   JitterBug

Dream in Color Yarns
907 Atlantic Ave.
West Chicago, IL 60185
(630)293-0123
dreamincoloryarns.com
   Smooshy

Fiesta Yarns
5401 San Diego NE
Albuquerque, NM 87113
(505) 892-5008
fiestayarns.com
   Baby Boom

Koigu Wool Designs
PO Box 158
Chatsworth, ON
Canada N0H1G0
(888) 765-WOOL
(519) 794-3066
koigu.com
   *Koigu Painter's Palette
   Premium Merino*
   Koigu Premium Merino

Lorna's Laces
4229 North Honore St.
Chicago, IL 60613
(773) 935-3803
lornaslaces.net
   Shepherd Sock

Mountain Colors
PO Box 156
Corvallis, MT 59828
(406) 961-1900
mountaincolors.com
   Bearfoot

Pagewood Farms
San Pedro, CA
(310) 403-7880
pagewoodfarm.com
   Chugiak

Schaefer Yarn Company
3514 Kelly's Corners Rd.
Interlaken, NY 14847
(607) 532-9452
schaeferyarn.com
   Anne

ShibuiKnits
1101 SW Alder St.
Portland, OR 97205
(503) 595-5898
shibuiknits.com
   Sock

bibliography

Bordhi, Cat. *Socks Soar on Two Circular Needles: A Manual of Elegant Knitting Techniques and Patterns*. Friday Harbor, Washington: Passing Paws Press, 2001.

Budd, Ann. *Getting Started Knitting Socks*. Loveland, Colorado: Interweave, 2007.

Budd, Ann, and Anne Merrow, eds. *Favorite Socks: 25 Timeless Designs from Interweave*. Loveland, Colorado: Interweave, 2007.

Bush, Nancy. *Folk Socks: The History & Techniques of Handknitted Footwear*. Loveland, Colorado: Interweave, 1994.

———. *Knitting on the Road: Sock Patterns for the Traveling Knitter*. Loveland, Colorado: Interweave, 2001.

———. *Knitting Vintage Socks: New Twists on Classic Patterns*. Loveland, Colorado: Interweave, 2004.

Galeskas, Bev. *The Magic Loop: Working Around on One Needle*. East Wenatchee, Washington: Fiber Trends, 2002.

Gibson-Roberts, Priscilla. *Simple Socks: Plain and Fancy*. Cedaredge, Colorado: Nomad Press, 2001.

Malcolm, Trish, et al. *Vogue Knitting: The Ultimate Sock Book: History, Technique, Design*. New York: Sixth & Spring Publishing, 2007.

Menz, Deb. *ColorWorks: The Crafter's Guide to Color*. Loveland, Colorado: Interweave, 2004.

Nicholas, Kristin. *Kristin Knits: 27 Inspired Designs for Playing with Color*. North Adams, Massachusetts: Storey Publishing, 2007.

Schurch, Charlene. *Sensational Knitted Socks*. Woodinville, Washington: Martingale & Co., 2005.

contributors

Véronik Avery is the author of *Classic Knitting Style*. Her designs have appeared in *Interweave Knits*, *Vogue Knitting* and books including *Lace Style*, *Handknit Holidays*, and *Wrap Style*. She lives in Montréal, where she is working on her second book.

Deb Barnhill has designed patterns for *Knitty.com* and *Alpacas Magazine*. A knitter since childhood, she lives in Nova Scotia and blogs at knittingpharm.com.

Barb Brown is a lifelong knitter with a particular passion for socks, as they are the one place that even a shy dresser can let loose. She lives near Cold Lake, Alberta, Canada, and owns Wild Geese Fibres.

Ann Budd, a book editor for Interweave, is a former senior editor of *Interweave Knits*. She is author of *The Knitter's Handy Book* series and *Getting Started Knitting Socks*, and coauthor of *Wrap Style, Lace Style, Bag Style*, and *Color Style*. She lives in Boulder, Colorado.

Chrissy Gardiner is owner of Gardiner Yarn Works, a wholesale pattern company. Her designs regularly appear in *Interweave Knits* and can be found in various books and yarn company patterns. She lives in Oregon.

Priscilla Gibson-Roberts is a passionate knitter of all things, but most especially socks. She studies the old ways of spinning and knitting, resulting in five books; she is currently working on her second book on Eastern ethnic socks.

Pam Grushkin has been an avid knitter for decades. She works at a Connecticut yarn shop, where she shares her passion for knitting through teaching and designing. She blogs at stitchandchat.blogspot.com.

Courtney Kelley is a knitwear and crochet designer who divides her time between Philadelphia and Smith Island, Maryland. She is the manager of Rosie's Yarn Cellar and co-owner of Kelbourne Woolens, distributor of The Fibre Company yarns.

Lorna Miser founded Lorna's Laces in 1985; although the company has changed hands, she enjoys designing for hand-dyed yarns and teaching. Her designs have been published by many yarn companies and publications. She is currently at work on a book.

Laura Nelkin has a degree in apparel design and worked in the fashion industry until she learned to knit. She became design director for Schaefer Yarn Company so she could be around fiber all the time.

Beth Parrott is from Charleston, South Carolina, where she knits, spins, felts, and dyes. She has been knitting for more than sixty years. She is the coauthor of *The Little Box of Socks*.

Jody Pirrello is a lifelong knitter, longtime knit blogger, and the founder of *Knotions.com*, an online knitting magazine. She lives in the Philadelphia suburbs of New Jersey.

Elizabeth Ravenwood is the author of *Knitting Languages, Knitted Snowflakes*, and other books and articles on fiber arts. When she's not teaching fiber arts workshops nationwide, she lives in Georgia.

Kristi Schueler designs knitwear and creates art in such diverse media as collage, bookmaking, soft block printing, and digital art. She lives in Colorado, where she blogs at blog.designedlykristi.com.

Charlene Schurch is the author of six knitting books: *Mostly Mittens, Hats On!, Knits for Girls and Dolls, Sensational Knitted Socks, More Sensational Knitted Socks*, and *Little Box of Socks*.

Mindy Soucek is a knitter, spinner, and designer who lives on a farm outside Madison, Virginia. She raises mohair goats and Angora rabbits.

Carol J. Sulcoski is a former attorney turned knitting designer and handdyer. She is a coauthor of *Knit So Fine* (Interweave). She lives outside Philadelphia.

index

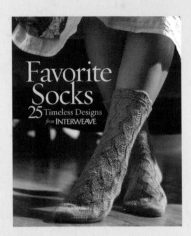